a different mirror
FOR YOUNG PEOPLE

A History of Multicultural America

Ronald Takaki

Adapted by Rebecca Stefoff

Seven Stories Press
Triangle Square Books for Young Readers
New York • Oakland • London

A Triangle Square *Books for young readers* edition,
published by Seven Stories Press.

SEVEN STORIES PRESS
140 Watts Street, New York, NY 10013
www.sevenstories.com

College professors and high school and middle school teachers may
order free examination copies of Seven Stories Press titles. To order,
visit www.sevenstories.com or send a fax on school
letterhead to (212) 226-1411.

Library of Congress Cataloging-in-Publication Data

Stefoff, Rebecca, 1951-
A different mirror for young people : a young people's history of mul-
ticultural America / by Ronald Takaki ; adapted by Rebecca Stefoff.
p. cm.
Includes bibliographical references and index.
ISBN 978-1-60980-484-8 (hbk. : alk. paper) --
ISBN 978-1-60980-416-9 (pbk. : alk. paper)
ISBN 978-1-60980-930-0 (library edition)

1., Minorities--United States--History--Juvenile literature. 2., United
States--Race relations--Juvenile literature. 3., United States--Ethnic
relations--Juvenile literature. 4., Cultural pluralism--United States-
-History--Juvenile literature., I. Takaki, Ronald T., 1939-2009. Different mirror. II. Title.
E184.A1T335 2012
305.800973--dc23
2012017004

Printed in the USA

13 15 17 19 20 18 16 14

Dedicated to our grandchildren—
Nicholas, Alexis, Zoë, Cooper, and Mia Takaki;
Rachael and Tanner Aikens

MY STORY, OUR STORY

I WAS GOING TO BE A SURFER, not a scholar.

I was born and grew up in Hawaii, the son
of a Japanese immigrant father and a Japanese-
American mother who had been born on a
sugarcane plantation. We lived in a working-class
neighborhood where my playmates were Japanese,
Chinese, Portuguese, Korean, and Hawaiian. We
did not use the word multicultural, but that's what
we were: a community of people from many cultural, national, and racial backgrounds.

My father died when I was five, and my mother
remarried a Chinese cook. She had gone to school
only through the eighth grade, and my stepfather
had very little education, but they were determined
to give me a chance to go to college. My passion as a
teenager, though, was surfing. My nickname was "Ten
Toes Takaki," and when I sat on my board and gazed
at rainbows over the mountains and the spectacular
sunsets over the Pacific, I wanted to be a surfer forever.

Then, during my senior year in high school, a teacher inspired me to think about the problems of the world and of being human and to ask, "How do you know what you know?" In other words, how do you know if something is true? The same teacher inspired me to attend college outside Hawaii, which is how I found myself at the College of Wooster in Ohio in 1957.

College was a culture shock for me. The student body was not very diverse, and my fellow students asked me, "How long have you been in this country? Where did you learn to speak English?" To them, I did not look like an American or have an American-sounding name. When I fell in love with one of those students, Carol Rankin, she told me that her parents would never approve of our relationship, because of my race.

Carol was right. Her parents were furious. Still, we decided to do what was right for us. When we got married, her parents reluctantly attended. Four years later, when our first child was born, her parents came to visit us in California. After I said, "Let me help you with the luggage, Mr. Rankin," Carol's father replied, "You can call me Dad." His racist attitudes, it turned out, were not frozen. He had changed.

By that time I was working on my Ph.D. degree in American history. I became a college professor at the University of California in Los Angeles and taught the school's first course in African American history. In 1971, I moved to the University of California at Berkeley to teach in a new Department of Ethnic Studies. In the decades that followed, I developed courses and degree programs in comparative ethnic studies, and I wrote several books about America's multicultural history. My extended family, too, became a multicultural, mixed-race group that now includes people of Japanese, Vietnamese, English, Chinese, Taiwanese, Jewish, and Mexican heritage.

I have come to see that my story reflects the story of multicultural America—a story of disappointments and dreams, struggles and triumphs, and identities that are separate but also shared. We must remember the histories of every group, for together they tell the story of a nation peopled by the world. As the time approaches when all Americans will be minorities, we face a challenge: not just to understand the world, but to make it better. A Different Mirror studies the past for the sake of the future.

CHAPTER ONE

WHY A DIFFERENT MIRROR?

I ONCE FLEW FROM San Francisco to Norfolk, Virginia, to give a speech at a teachers' conference on multicultural education. In the taxi on the way to the conference, the driver, a white man in his forties, chatted with me about the weather. Then he asked, "How long have you been in this country?"

The question made me wince, even though I had heard it many times before.

"All my life," I said. "I was born in the United States."

"I was wondering because your English is excellent!" he replied. He glanced at me in his rearview mirror. To him, I did not look like an American.

Feeling suddenly awkward, we fell silent. I looked at the Virginia scenery and thought about how our route was taking us through the beginning of multicultural America.

Here, on land taken from the Indians, English

(left, detail)
Arrival of
a Dutch slave ship
at Jamestown,
Virginia, 1619.

colonizers founded the settlement of Jamestown in 1607. After they discovered that great profit could be made by growing tobacco and shipping it to England, they wanted more Indian land— and people to work it. In 1619, a year before the English Pilgrims landed at Plymouth Rock in Massachusetts, a Dutch slave ship arrived at Jamestown, bringing the first twenty African laborers to the American colonies. From the beginning, this land was multiracial and multicultural.

But it was not my taxi driver's fault that he did not see me as a fellow citizen. What had he learned about Asian Americans in his school courses on US history? He saw me through a filter—a version of American history that I call the "Master Narrative."

Challenging the "Master Narrative"

The Master Narrative says that our country was settled by European immigrants, and that Americans are white. People of other races, people not of European ancestry, have been pushed to the sidelines of the Master Narrative. Sometimes they are ignored completely. Sometimes they are merely treated as the "Other"—different and inferior.

Either way, they are not seen as part of America's national identity.

The Master Narrative is a powerful story, and a popular one. It is deeply embedded in our culture, in the writings of many scholars, and in the ways people teach and talk about American history. But the Master Narrative is inaccurate. Its definition of who is an American is too narrow.

Harvard historian Oscar Handlin was one of many scholars who followed the Master Narrative. In his prize-winning book *The Uprooted*, about "the epic story of the great migrations that made the American people," Handlin wrote about immigrants—but only those who came to the United States from Europe. His "epic story" overlooked Native Americans, as well as people who came from Africa, Asia, and Latin America.

Things have changed since Handlin's book was published in 1951. Our expanding racial diversity is challenging the Master Narrative. Demography, which is the study of population trends, is declaring: Not all of us came originally from Europe!

A third of Americans today trace their ancestry to somewhere other than Europe. In California, blacks, Latinos, Asian Americans, and Native Americans have become the majority. Minorities outnumber whites in cities across the country, such as Boston, New York, Chicago, Atlanta, Detroit, Houston, San Francisco, and Los Angeles. Within the lifetime of young people today, people of European descent will become a minority in the United States. We will all be minorities.

How can we prepare ourselves for this future? One way is to recover the missing chapters of American history. We must study our diversity to understand how and why America became what poet Walt Whitman called a "teeming nation of nations."

The change is already happening. In recent decades, many school systems and colleges have added multicultural studies to give students a more diverse and complete education. Scholars and historians, meanwhile, have delved into the experiences of various immigrant and minority groups.

A More Inclusive History

An even bigger picture of race and ethnicity in America comes from looking at many groups comparatively. Although it would be impossible to cover all racial and ethnic groups in one book, *A*

Different Mirror focuses on African, Asian, Irish, Jewish, Latino, Mexican, Muslim, and Native Americans. Woven together, the experiences of these minorities show how the landscape of our society's diversity was formed.

African Americans have been the central minority throughout our country's history. At first, the English plantation owners in the colonies preferred white workers, for they wanted their new society to be all white. But after an armed uprising by the workers in 1676, the elite or upper-class colonists turned to Africa for their main supply of laborers, who would be enslaved and prevented from owning guns.

After the Civil War ended slavery, a grim future awaited African Americans: racial segregation, lynchings, and race riots. Still, they insistently struggled for freedom and equality. Joined by people of other races in the civil rights movement of the 1960s, African Americans won significant victories that changed society. The history of African Americans has been stitched into the history of America itself. Martin Luther King, Jr., clearly understood this when he wrote from a jail cell, "We will reach the goal of freedom . . . all over the nation, because the goal of America is freedom.

Abused and scorned though we may be, our destiny is tied up with America's destiny."

Asian Americans began arriving in America long before many European immigrants. The Chinese came as gold prospectors and railroad builders. Later they became farm and factory workers. Although the Chinese were wanted as

temporary laborers, they were not welcomed as permanent settlers. During an economic depression, Congress passed the Chinese Exclusion Act of 1882, the first law that prevented immigrants from entering the United States based on their nationality.

The Japanese also painfully discovered that their accomplishments in America did not lead to acceptance. In the 1940s, during World War II, the government sent 120,000 Japanese Americans to camps where they were guarded like prisoners. Two-thirds of them were US citizens. "How could I as a six-month-old child born in this country," asked Congressman Robert Matsui years later, "be declared by my own Government to be an enemy alien?"

Another wave of Asian immigrants arrived in 1975, when tens of thousands of Vietnamese fled to America to escape the Vietnam War. Joined by arrivals from Korea, the Philippines, India, Cambodia, Laos, and other countries, Asian Americans have become one of the fastest-growing ethnic groups in the United States, projected to reach 10 percent of the population by 2050.

In the nineteenth century, a wave of Irish immigrants arrived—four million of them,

(left) Arrival of a Dutch slave ship at Jamestown, Virginia, 1619.

driven out of their native land by starvation and homelessness. Because they were Catholics who wanted to settle in a fiercely Protestant society, the Irish became victims of hostility and prejudice. Because they were white, however, the Irish could become American citizens, unlike Asian immigrants. (Under a law called the 1790 Naturalization Act, only white immigrants could apply for citizenship.) By 1900, the Irish were entering the middle class.

Many Jews came to the United States from Russia because they were fleeing pogroms, or organized massacres by the non-Jewish majority in Russia. Jews settled into the Lower East Side of Manhattan, in New York City—a beehive of crowded apartment buildings and garment factories where Jewish women worked.

To these Jews, America represented the Promised Land. This vision energized them to rise into the middle class by emphasizing education. But in the 1930s, as Jewish immigrants and their children were entering the mainstream of American society, they found themselves facing the rise of German leader Adolph Hitler and the ultimate pogrom: the Holocaust, Hitler's mass killing of millions of European Jews and other minorities.

When American Jews demanded that the United States do everything possible to rescue people destined for Hitler's death camps, they were met with a lack of interest or even with anti-Semitism, which is prejudice against Jewish people. The result was a strong wave of Jewish American activism for human rights and social justice.

Mexican Americans first became part of the United States in 1848, when the United States won a war with Mexico. These Mexicans did not immigrate into America, however. Instead, the US border was moved. People living in what had been the northern part of Mexico suddenly found themselves living in California and the southwestern territories of the United States.

Most Mexican Americans today, though, have immigrant roots. The trek of Mexicans to *El Norte*—"the North," or the United States—began in the early twentieth century. Mexican Americans have had a different experience from other immigrants because their homeland borders the United States. That closeness has helped them maintain their language, ethnic identity, and traditional culture.

Mexicans still cross the border from the south, seeking to escape poverty and find work. Most of the nation's "illegal aliens"—as non-citizens in the United States without proper paperwork have been called—are from Mexico. A burning political question is: What to do with them? Yet many Mexican Americans, like members of other groups, have been learning English, applying for citizenship, voting, and becoming Americans.

Like the Mexicans who lived in the Southwest when it was conquered by the United States, the people of the Caribbean island of Puerto Rico had American citizenship thrust upon them. Puerto Rico became a colony of the United States in 1898, and in 1917 an act of Congress granted citizenship to all Puerto Ricans, although they cannot vote in presidential elections.

Puerto Ricans have been migrating from their island to the US mainland since the middle of the twentieth century. At the time of the 2010 census, 4.7 million Puerto Ricans were living in the States—nearly a million more than lived in Puerto Rico. Along with immigrants from other Caribbean islands such as Jamaica, Cuba, Trinidad, Guadeloupe, and the Dominican Republic, Puerto Ricans make up a significant presence in many communities, especially in East Coast cities such as New York.

Muslim Americans have been coming to the United States from many countries, but those who came as refugees from the war-torn western Asian nation of Afghanistan have faced unique difficulties. The Afghan refugees were hardly noticed in America until September 11, 2001, when terrorist attacks on the World Trade Center and the Pentagon suddenly changed their lives.

The terrorists were traced to a group called Al-Qaeda, based in Afghanistan. While Western powers led by the United States invaded Afghanistan, seeking to destroy Al-Qaeda, Afghan Americans lived with the fear of anti-Muslim prejudice and violence, and with the knowledge that a return to their homeland was unlikely.

Native Americans are different from all other groups within United States society. Theirs was not an immigrant experience—the native Indians were the original Americans, here for thousands of years before Europeans arrived. The Europeans labeled them "savages" and seized their lands by force, first along the eastern shore of the continent, and eventually westward all the way to the Pacific Ocean. Soldiers who led military campaigns against the Indians were honored as heroes.

Whites saw controlling the Indians as progress, but the Indians had a different view. As Luther Standing Bear of the Sioux nation said, "The white man does not understand the Indian for the reason that he does not understand America. The man from Europe is still a foreigner and an alien."

Conflicts and Shared Dreams

As these groups met and mingled in America, seeking work and a place in society, they often were swept into ethnic conflicts. In the nineteenth century, for example, hostility flared between African Americans and Irish immigrants.

The Irish were viewed by mainstream Protestant society as ignorant and inferior, and they had to settle for the worst, lowest-paying jobs. In the North, Irish workers competed with blacks to become waiters or laborers on shipping docks. In the South, they did jobs considered too dangerous to be done by slaves, who were regarded as valuable property by their owners.

The Irish complained that blacks did not know their place. A common cry among the Irish was, "Let them go back to Africa, where they belong!" Blacks born in America, however, complained that the Irish newcomers were taking jobs from them. The Irish "are crowding themselves into every place of business and labor," one African American complained, "and driving the poor colored American citizen out."

In spite of competition and hostility, though, minorities have also had much in common. They have shared similar hopeful dreams of the good life in America. An Irish immigrant woman wrote home to her father about "this plentiful Country where no man or woman ever hungered." A Japanese man said of his decision to come to the United States:

> *Day of spacious dreams!*
> *I sailed for America,*
> *Overblown with hope.*

And Jews in Russia, eager to escape the violence, sang of their dream:

> *As the Russians mercilessly*
> *Took revenge on us,*
> *There is a land, America,*
> *Where everyone lives free.*

No matter what minority group they belonged to, workers shared another experience as well— the experience of being exploited, or being taken advantage of, by factory owners and other bosses. Sometimes the workers rose above their racial and ethnic differences, uniting in strikes for better pay or better working conditions. In 1903 in California, Mexican and Japanese farm laborers went on strike together. Japanese and Filipino laborers did the same in Hawaii in 1920. During the 1930s, the labor union known as the Committee for Industrial Organization (CIO) called for "absolute racial equality in Union membership." This kind of cooperation showed that differences do not have to keep people apart.

America's Epic Story

The people of multicultural America have sometimes been reluctant to speak, thinking they were only "little people." As an Irish maid said in 1900, "I don't know why anybody wants to hear my story." But people's stories are worthy. Native American writer Leslie Marmon Silko explains why:

I will tell you something about stories . . .
They aren't just entertainment.
Don't be fooled.

The stories of minorities capture not just
moments of history but also powerful emotions and
thoughts. After she escaped from slavery, Harriet
Jacobs wrote, "[My purpose] is not to tell you what I
have heard but what I have seen—and what I have
suffered." A Chinese immigrant hoped in 1920 that
his story would help Americans "realize that Chinese people are human." And a Jewish immigrant
dedicated her autobiography to "the descendants
of Lazar and Goldie Glauberman," in the hope that
future generations would "know where they came
from to know better who they are."

But what happens when historians do not
record these stories, leaving out many of America's peoples? An incomplete history is like a
mirror that does not reflect everything, a mirror
that treats some people as if they were invisible.
But it is possible to hold up a different mirror to
history. That different mirror reflects everyone's
history. It lets us glimpse the nation that the poet
Langston Hughes described:

Let America be America again.

. . . .,

Let America be the dream the dreamers
dreamed—

. . . .,

O, let my land be a land where. . .

. . . .,

Equality is in the air we breathe.

. . . .,

Say who are you that mumbles in the dark?

. . . .,

I am the poor white, fooled and pushed apart,
I am the Negro bearing slavery's scars.
I am the red man driven from the land,
I am the immigrant clutching the hope I
seek—

The struggle to "let America be America" has
been this nation's epic story. The original inhabitants were joined by people who were pushed
from their homelands by poverty and persecution, or pulled to a new land by their dreams.
Others came here in chains from Africa, and still
others fled as refugees from wars in countries
like Vietnam and Afghanistan. All of them were
part of the making of multicultural America, a

process that began when Europeans first landed
on American shores.

ONE STORY,
MANY SONGS

ONE OF THE GREATEST ACHIEVEMENTS OF
American industry in the nineteenth century was
the transcontinental railroad. Together the Chinese
workers of the Central Pacific and the Irish of the
Union Pacific laid this ribbon of steel that connected the nation's two coasts. It became part of a
network of railroads that moved people, raw materials, and goods throughout the entire country.

The building of the US railway system required
the labor of people from many racial and ethnic
backgrounds. Different as these people were, their
work songs told the story of shared experiences.

Black laborers sang as they laid railroad ties:

> *Down the railroad, um-huh,*
> *Well, raise the iron, um-huh,*
> *Raise the iron, um-huh.*

Irish workers shouted as the sweat on their
backs shone in the sun:

> *Then drill, my Paddies, drill—*

Drill, my heroes, drill,
Drill all day, no sugar in your tay [tea]
Workin' on the UP railway.

Japanese laborers sang as they fought the changeable weather of the Northwest:

A railroad worker—
That's me!
I am great.
Yes, I am a railroad worker.
Complaining:
"It is too hot!"
"It is too cold!"
"It rains too often!"
"It snows too much!"
They all ran off.
I alone remained.
I am a railroad worker.

And in the Southwest, Mexican American laborers added their voices to the chorus of songs about the hard, hard work:

Some unloaded rails
Others unloaded ties,
And others of my companions
Threw out thousands of curses.

REMOVING THE "SAVAGES"

MORE THAN A THOUSAND years ago, a meeting took place on the edge of North America. On the shore stood Beothuk, Native Americans who lived along what is now the eastern coast of Canada. From the sea came longships filled with tall strangers who had pale skin, yellow hair, and blue eyes. The meeting ended in bloodshed. The strangers killed the Indians—all but one, who escaped in his small skin-covered boat.

The strangers were Norsemen, Vikings from Greenland who had originally come from Norway. Their leader was Thorvald Eiriksson, the brother of Leif Eiriksson. On a voyage from Iceland around the year 1000, Leif had become the first European to reach North America. Thorvald and his men had followed Leif's directions to the new land, where they had fought with the first people they met.

(left, detail) Woodcut showing Indian walled town, like those of the Powhatans near Jamestown.

After Thorvald and the others made camp, they were attacked in their sleep by a band of Beothuk. Thorvald died of his wounds, but that did not stop another group of Vikings from trying to settle in the place they called Vinland. Before long, though, the Vikings abandoned Vinland and returned to Greenland. They realized that "although this was a good country, there would always be terror and trouble from the people who lived there." The Viking settlement in North America remained little more than a legend until 1960, when the remains of thousand-year-old Viking buildings were found on the Canadian island of Newfoundland.

Almost five hundred years later, another group of Europeans landed in North America. A Spanish expedition commanded by Christopher Columbus reached the islands of the Caribbean Sea. Columbus had planned to sail to Asia. He believed he had succeeded, but in reality he had bumped into lands unknown to Europeans. This accident of history opened the way for Spain, Portugal, France, Holland, and England to send explorers, soldiers, and colonists to the continents that would be named the Americas.

Unlike the Vikings, these new strangers stayed.

English Over Irish

English colonists settled in Virginia in 1607 and Massachusetts in 1620. Just as had happened to the Vikings, the English found Native American peoples living in the "new land" they wanted to make home. In deciding how to deal with the Indians, the English used a method they had already practiced on another frontier.

England's other frontier was Ireland. In both Ireland and America, the English were interacting with people they saw as "Other," different from themselves. And in both places, the English drew a line between "civilization" and "savagery"—a line that defined the English as civilized and the Others as savage.

In the late sixteenth century, shortly before the beginning of the English migrations to North America, England's Queen Elizabeth I encouraged some of her subjects to colonize Ireland, an island just west of England. The queen's advisers warned her that Ireland posed a threat. It was a Catholic nation, and more powerful Catholic countries such as Spain or France might use it as a base from which to attack England.

Elizabeth's chosen soldiers included Sir Humphrey Gilbert and Sir Walter Raleigh. Like many

English people, these two were Protestants who believed that the Irish Catholics were not just savages but also pagans, or people who were not even Christians. To the English, the Irish were also completely lacking in "good manners," good work habits, and a proper sense of private property.

The English colonizers in Ireland set up a two-level social structure. Irish people were forbidden to wear English-style clothes or carry English weapons, on pain of death. No Irish could own property, hold public office, or serve on a jury. To reinforce this social separation, the English outlawed marriage between the Irish and their colonizers. The new world order was to be one of English over Irish.

The Irish also became targets of English violence, especially during the Nine Years' War, which began in 1594. "Nothing but fear and force can teach duty and obedience to such rebellious people," the invaders insisted. The English burned Irish villages and crops, moving the people onto reservations. Whole families were slaughtered, but the English justified their actions by saying that the families provided support for the rebels.

The invaders took the heads of their slain enemies as trophies. Sir Humphrey Gilbert ordered that the path to his tent on the battlefield should be lined with these trophies, so that anyone who came to see him must "pass through a lane of heads."

The high death toll of the Irish soon left the land almost empty, which to the English meant that it was vacant and ready for them to settle it. And the same awful acts that had been committed against the Irish would soon be committed against the Native Americans, often by English veterans of the war in Ireland.

English over Indians

Even before the English began colonizing America, they viewed the Native American people as savage, even, sometimes, as less than human. They had heard about the Indians, and some had seen them. Ever since Columbus gave six captive Indians to the Spanish king and queen after his voyage, along with some gold nuggets and parrots, sea captains who sailed to the Americas had been kidnapping Indians and carrying them across the ocean to be displayed as curiosities.

In 1605 Captain George Waymouth sailed along the coast of New England. He lured Abenaki

Indians onto his ship and kidnapped three of them. Another account boasted of having shipped back to England "five savages, two canoes, with all their bows and arrows." And in 1611 an Indian was brought to England and, because he was tall, "was showed up and down London for money as a monster."

Those who displayed these Native Americans presented them as "cruel, barbarous, and most treacherous." A writer named Richard Johnson described them in 1609 as "wild and savage people" who lived "like herds of deer in the forest."

When the first English colonizers arrived in the Americas, they found that the houses, clothes, and customs of the Native American people reminded them of "the wild Irish." From the start, the English viewed the Americas in terms of their experiences in the Old World. Because they saw the Irish as "savages," when they compared the Indians to the Irish, they were defining the Indians as savages, too.

Originally, planners in London expected the English colonists to "civilize" the savages by taking their Indian children from them and to "train them up with gentleness, teach them our English language." In the 1606 contract with the Virginia

Company that founded Jamestown, King James I supported a plan to teach Christianity to the Indians. Publicity for the colony said that the savage Indians could and should be educated, which would civilize them.

What would happen to these ideas about American "savages," and to the plans for "civilizing" them, when Indians and English colonizers faced each other?

Virginia Aims to "Root Out" Native People

At the Jamestown colony in Virginia, the English found themselves living in the ancestral homeland of about fourteen thousand Powhatan Indians. The Powhatan were farmers who cultivated corn and lived in walled towns, where the buildings were covered with tree bark and mats made of reeds. They cooked in ceramic pottery and wove baskets so fine that some of them could hold water.

The first encounters between the English and the Powhatan opened possibilities for friendship and cooperation. The original 120 colonizers were poorly prepared for survival in the American wilderness. They found conditions so harsh that one of them, John Smith, called their first year "the starving time." At the end of it only thirty-eight remained, hanging onto the edge of survival, and "expecting every hour the fury of the savages," as Smith wrote. The Indians did come, but instead of fury they brought food and rescued the starving strangers.

Several hundred more settlers arrived from England. Again, they soon ran out of provisions. They had to eat "dogs, cats, rates, and mice," and some turned to cannibalism. The English tried to force the Powhatans to give them food by attacking them and burning their villages.

Relations between the two peoples got worse after a new governor arrived with orders that the Indians must make yearly payments of corn and deerskins to the colonists and also work for them. These orders were brutally carried out. The English burned Indian villages and fields. One commander, George Percy, described killing Indian children by "throwing them overboard and shooting out their brains in the water." The Indians came to doubt that the two peoples could live together in peace. They felt the newcomers were determined to take their land.

Within a few years the Jamestown colonists

discovered a profitable new business—growing tobacco for export. To expand their tobacco farms they wanted more land, especially land that the Powhatan had already cleared for their own farms. Tobacco farming, in turn, drew more immigrants to the colony. In just five years, from 1618 to 1623, the population of Jamestown grew from 400 to 4,500.

The Indians tried to drive out the intruders, killing some three hundred colonists in an attack that Smith called a "massacre" by "cruel beasts." These deaths made the English feel that they had a right to the land—that it had been bought with English blood. They decided to "destroy them who sought to destroy us" and take over the Indians' towns and farms.

The war against the Indians was vicious and treacherous. The English rode down the Powhatan on horseback and chased them with dogs. They starved them by burning their food. A captain named William Tucker went to a Powhatan village to make a peace treaty. After they signed the treaty, he persuaded the Indians to drink a toast—then served them poisoned wine, killing an estimated two hundred. Tucker's soldiers "brought home parts of their heads" as trophies.

By 1629 the goal of the English in Virginia was no longer to civilize or educate the Indians. It was to "root out [the Indians] from being any longer a people."

New England Turns Indians into Demons

John Smith had sailed north from Virginia in 1616 to explore the New England coast. The "paradise" of Massachusetts, he reported, was "all planted with corn, groves, mulberries, savage gardens." Indeed, the Native Americans of the New England coast—the Wampanoag, Pequot, Narragansett, and others—were farmers. They grew corn, beans, and pumpkins, and they planted groves of chestnut and hickory trees to supply their communities with nuts. This way of life brought them into competition with the English Pilgrims who founded a colony at Plymouth Rock in 1620, and then with the Puritans who soon settled on Massachusetts Bay.

New England is hilly and rocky. Less than 20 percent of the area in the English colonies was good for farming—and the Indians already occupied the best areas. At first the English managed to take over those lands without fighting because Indians had died in massive numbers from European diseases such as smallpox. William Bradford, who led the Pilgrims to Plymouth Rock, wrote in his diary, "For it pleased God to visit these Indians with a great sickness and such a mortality that of a thousand, above nine and a half hundred of them died, and many of them did rot above ground for want of burial."

(left) Woodcut showing Indian walled town, like those of the Powhatans near Jamestown.

The colonizers saw the Indian deaths as a sign that God had given the land to them—God was "making room" for the settlers. Indian death did mean life for the Pilgrims, who owed their survival to a store of corn they had found among Indian graves on Cape Cod. Later, many New England towns were founded on the very places where Indians had lived before the epidemics of disease wiped them out.

As the English population grew, the settlers needed even more land. To justify taking it from the Native Americans who had survived, the English argued that the Indians did not deserve the land because they were lazy and did not work as hard as the English did. Ignoring the evidence that Indians had been farmers in New England, the English compared the Indians to "foxes and wild beasts" who did nothing "but run over the grass."

Over the years, the growth of the English settlements led to wars. During the Pequot War of 1637, the English and their Indian allies killed some seven hundred Pequot, burning many of them—including women and children—in their forts. Nearly forty years later the Indians struck back at the colonists in King Philip's War, which nearly succeeded in driving the English out of New England. Reinforced by troops from England, however, the settlers overcame the Indians, killing and enslaving thousands.

Religious leaders led the way in justifying violence against the Native Americans. Ministers talked of the war against the Indians as a battle between God and the Devil. Cotton Mather called the Indians "miserable savages" who worshipped the Devil. The Puritan colonists in Massachusetts were strict Protestants who believed in witchcraft. They claimed that some of the colonists whom they accused of witchcraft had been encouraged by demons in the form of Indians.

Not everyone in the English settlements saw the Native Americans as completely demons or animals. Mary Rowlandson had been captured by the Narragansett during King Philip's War. She lived with them for eleven weeks. In 1682, after she had returned to white society, she published a book about her experiences with the Indians.

Rowlandson's story echoed many English stereotypes of the Indians as "barbarous creatures," "merciless and cruel," and "hellhounds." At the same time, some parts of her story challenged these negative images. Indians had treated her and her six-year-old daughter with kindness and generosity, she reported. They were also generous with each other. She wrote, "I did not see (all the time I was among them) one man, woman, or child, dy[die] with hunger."

By recognizing the humanity of the Indians, Rowlandson's story offered a chance for the English to understand, or even share the feelings of, the people whose land they were taking. But the English did not pursue this chance. Instead, they continued their relentless conquest of the North American continent.

Stolen Lands and a World Turned "Upside Down"

During the eighteenth century, the English colonies in North America grew larger in population and developed thriving economies. Eventually they fought for independence, and after they had won it, they joined to form the United States of America. Cities and towns expanded, settlers moved westward, and the new nation seemed set on a path of prosperity and progress.

Progress for white Americans, however, led to poverty for Native Americans. In 1789 the Mohegan tribe sent a message to the government of Connecticut, lamenting their hardships. "[T]he Times have turn'd everything Upside down," said the message.

Once, the Mohegan had had plenty of game, fish, and crops, and no need to fight over land. "But alas, it is not so now." The Indians had begun to live like white people, with horses and cattle and fenced lots, but there was no longer enough for all, "and poor Widows and Orphans Must be pushed one side and there they Must Set a Crying, Starving and die."

Ever since the arrival of the English, the Indians' story had been one of stolen lands, sickness, starvation, suffering, and sadness. After the War of

(left) Title page of the 1773 edition of Mary Rowlandson's book about her time as an Indian captive.

Independence and the founding of the new nation of the United States, the Native Americans wondered what the future would hold for them.

Another person who asked this question was one of the Founding Fathers—a lawyer, Virginia planter, and author of the Declaration of Independence. In 1781, as governor of Virginia, Thomas Jefferson had told the Kaskaskia tribe that whites and Indians were "both Americans, born in the same land," and that he hoped the two peoples would "long continue to smoke in friendship together." Other statements, however, revealed that Jefferson held a very different view.

In 1776, when the colonists began their War of Independence, Jefferson had supported removing, even destroying, hostile Indians. "Nothing will reduce those wretches so soon as pushing the war into the heart of their country," he wrote to a friend. "But I would not stop there. . . . We would never cease pursuing them with war while one remained on the face of the earth." In Jefferson's view, Indians had to be either civilized (in other words, made to act like white people) or exterminated.

Later, as president, Jefferson told the Cherokee people, "I shall rejoice to see the day when the red man, our neighbors, become truly one people with us, enjoying all the rights and privileges we do, and living in peace and plenty as we do." But in order to do that, Jefferson insisted, Native Americans must give up their customs, beliefs, and traditional ways of life. They must build fences, learn arithmetic, and live like whites.

Jefferson also promised the Indians that they could keep their own lands. "Your lands are your own; your right to them shall never be violated by us; they are yours to keep or sell as you please." Yet Jefferson worked to make it harder for Indians to refuse to sell land to whites. One way was to discourage Indians from hunting and make them take up farming. If they did not need the forests for hunting, Jefferson claimed, they would be more willing to sell them to whites. Another plan was to build more trading posts to sell white-manufactured goods to the Indians on credit. This would destroy the Indians financially. When the Indians found themselves in debt, they would have no choice but to hand over their land.

For Jefferson, the Indians could not be allowed to remain within society as Indians. In the seventeenth century, New Englanders had celebrated the disappearance of wolves and bears from their settlements. In 1824, the year he died, Jefferson wrote a letter that revealed his vision of America's future. He looked forward to the day when "wild beasts" and the "savages" who lived like them would be gone from the land, and "the advance of civilization" would be complete.

A SETTLER GIRL
BECOMES A SENECA

SOME OF AMERICA'S FIRST ADVENTURE TALES
were captivity narratives like Mary Rowlandson's.
These were the stories of white colonists who had
been captured by Native Americans. Captives who
escaped or were released would return to white
society and write or talk about their experiences.

Not all captives chose to return, however. Mary
Jemison is one of those who remained with the
Native Americans.

Mary was fifteen years old when, sometime
between 1755 and 1758, her family was captured by
a band of Shawnee Indians and French soldiers. At
the time, frontier wars in the American colonies pitted the English against the French and their Indian
allies. The Jemison family had settled on Indian
land in central Pennsylvania. Like other settlers
there, they were taken by the enemy. The Shawnees
killed Mary's parents and siblings but gave Mary to
members of the Seneca tribe, who adopted her as a
replacement for a young man who had been killed
in the fighting.

"During my adoption," Mary recalled years later,

"I sat motionless, nearly terrified to death at the appearance and actions of the company, expecting every moment to feel their vengeance, and suffer death on the spot. I was, however, happily disappointed, when at the close of the ceremony the company retired, and my [Indian] sisters went about employing every means for my consolation and comfort." She added, "I was very fortunate in falling into their hands; for they were kind good natured women; peaceable and mild in their dispositions; temperate and decent in their habits, and very tender and gentle toward me."

Mary married a Delaware Indian. They had a son, but Mary's husband died while the family was moving to a new home in New York State. Later Mary married a Seneca man, and they had six children together. They survived the American Revolution—although they sided with the British in that conflict—and Mary lived with the Seneca until her death at nearly ninety.

Mary's story is known to us because, when she was an old woman, she told it to a minister, James E. Seaver, who published it in 1824. Historians think *A Narrative of the Life of Mrs. Mary Jemison* is fairly accurate. Like the story of Mary Rowlandson more than a century earlier, Mary Jemison's story shows that in the clash between whites and Native Americans, there was right and wrong, and also gentleness and violence, on both sides.

THE HIDDEN ORIGINS OF SLAVERY

FOUR BARRELS OF TOBACCO arrived on a London shipping dock in 1613. This was the first shipment of tobacco from the English colony in Virginia. It would not be the last. The market for tobacco grew as fast as the plant itself. Just seven years after that first small shipment, the colony sent sixty thousand barrels of tobacco to London.

The growing demand for tobacco created a demand for labor. People were needed to clear the planters' new fields and to plant and tend the tobacco, which required a lot of backbreaking care during the growing season. Then came harvesting the leaves, hanging them on lines to dry out, and packing them into barrels for export.

If the land-owning colonists were to make fortunes from tobacco, they needed people to work their plantations. To meet that need, they created a complicated social structure in the Vir-

(left, detail) Violence erupted in the Virginia colony in what became known as Bacon's Rebellion, 1676.

ginia colony—one that led, in time, to slavery and rebellion.

Slave or Servant?

Twenty Africans arrived in the Jamestown colony in 1619, carried on a Dutch ship. They had probably been captured in wars or raids by enemy tribes before they were sold as slaves. These were the first blacks brought to the English North American colonies. Although they were not free, in Virginia they were not really slaves.

A slave is a person who is regarded as property under the law. Enslaved people belong to others and are required to work without pay for life, or until set free by their owners. In 1619 Virginia had no law making slavery legal. The twenty Africans who were brought by the Dutch ship were sold, but not as slaves. They were indentured servants, like many of the white laborers who were coming to the colony at that time.

An indentured servant was bound by law to work for a master for a set period of time, usually four to seven years. The servant owed this labor to the master because the master had paid for the servant's voyage to America, or had paid to acquire the servant from someone else (such as the Dutch shipmaster who brought the first twenty Africans). At the end of the indenture, or term of service, indentured servants were free to look for jobs, claim land of their own, or do whatever they could to support themselves.

English colonies outside North America relied heavily on African labor. The Caribbean island of Barbados, for example, had 20,000 black slaves by 1660, which meant that the majority of the island's population was black. But in Virginia the black population grew very slowly. In 1650 there were three hundred blacks in the colony, about 2 percent of the total population. Twenty-five years later the black population of Virginia numbered just sixteen hundred or 5 percent.

Why did the Virginia colonists import so few African workers, if they needed labor so badly? The answer lies in an important difference between the Barbados and Virginia colonies.

Most of the English planters in Barbados were businessmen who planned to make their fortunes on the island and then return to England. Most of the Virginia colonists, though, had brought their families with them. They planned to stay in America, and they wanted to create a reproduction of English society in Virginia. Because English society was white, they wanted Virginia society to remain white as well.

Three-quarters of the people who came to the Virginia colony before 1700 were indentured servants. Most of them were white. They came from England, Ireland, and Germany, from the poor classes and from society's outcasts: convicts, the homeless and jobless, people who could not pay their debts. Some were tricked into indenture, some were kidnapped, and some came voluntarily, driven by desperation or the dream of a fresh start. In Virginia they found themselves working alongside African servants.

Coming from different shores, the white and black laborers had limited understanding of each other. Still, they shared the same exploitation and abuse. Some servants had to wear iron collars. All had to show passes whenever they left the master's property. They were beaten and sometimes tortured, and many lived in miserable conditions with poor food. Indentured men and women of both races experienced the day-to-day exhaustion and harshness of plantation labor.

Blacks and whites sometimes joined forces. Servants of both races deserted their masters together so often that the Virginia legislature complained about the problem of "English servants running away with Negroes." Court records contain evidence of another kind of partnership—interracial sexual relationships, which were punished by whippings or public shaming of men and women.

Slavery Becomes Law

White and black servants shared many hardships, but over time blacks were singled out for different treatment. They were forbidden to use guns, although masters could arm their white servants. Periods of indenture were generally longer for blacks than for whites.

Punishments differed, too. In 1640 three runaway male servants were captured and returned to their masters. Two were white; one was black. Each man received thirty lashes from a whip. The whites each had one year added to their indentures, and in addition they were ordered to work for the colony for three more years after their indentures ended. But the black runaway, John Punch, was sentenced to servitude for life.

Legal documents from the seventeenth century show that when colonists sold or traded their servants, white servants were sold for their "full term of time" (the legal period of indenture) while blacks were sold "forever." In 1653 one colonist sold a ten-year-old black girl named Jowan to another colonist. The sale included any children Jowan might bear, and their children, and so on, forever.

Black servants were becoming property. They were not yet slaves under the law, but they were treated like slaves. Before long, the law was changed to make it official. In 1661 the Virginia legislature passed a law that allowed lifetime servitude, or slavery, for blacks. Eight years later another law defined a slave as property. The institution of slavery had taken root in North America.

Around the time African laborers were made slaves, the number of white indentured servants coming to Virginia started to drop. Yet the colony's planters did not rush to import more blacks—they still wanted to keep Virginia white. In the 1680s, though, the number of blacks brought into the colony increased. This sudden growth in the importing of blacks came about because of a class war that shook Virginia in the 1670s.

"Poore, Indebted, Discontented and Armed"

Most English colonists who came to Virginia did so as indentured servants. They planned to complete their term of service and become freemen. Then, by law, they could claim fifty acres of land and try to make their own profits by farming tobacco.

The high demand for tobacco, though, created a land boom. The richer colonists scrambled to buy up all the best land. This land-owning elite class controlled the legislature and passed laws to protect its own interests. For example, the legislature lengthened the term of indentured servitude for whites. This helped the elite class in two ways. It increased the supply of labor by keeping servants indentured for longer periods, and it reduced competition from freemen for land.

White freemen and indentured servants saw that it was becoming harder and harder to become landowners. Many of them grew angry, feeling that they had been tricked into coming to America. An unhappy underclass formed, made up of indentured servants, slaves, and landless freemen, both black and white. Their restlessness was shared by poor freemen who owned land, but who had been pushed onto land claims in the backcountry, far from rivers, roads, and markets.

This unruly underclass was a disturbing element in the social order. In the early 1660s an indentured servant named Isaac Friend plotted to band together with forty other servants, get hold of weapons, and claim their freedom by killing anyone who opposed them. Authorities learned of the plot and crushed

the rebellion before it started. In 1663 a Virginia court accused nine laborers of another plot, this time to overthrow the government of the colony. Several of the accused men were executed.

The elite class was so afraid of the landless rabble that in 1670 the Virginia legislature took steps to rein in the political power of the poor. The legislature passed a law saying that only men who owned land could vote. But although voting was limited to property owners, guns were not. Colony law required every white man to have a gun for use in defending the colony from attack.

William Berkeley, the governor of Virginia, feared that conditions were growing explosive in his colony. Six out of seven people, he wrote, were "Poore, Indebted, Discontented and Armed." Free-men and debtors could not be trusted in battle, the governor warned. They might revolt and join forces with the enemy.

Bacon's Rebellion

Governor Berkeley's fears came true in 1676 at the hands of Nathaniel Bacon, a tobacco planter in the backcountry. Bacon was concerned about Indian attacks on settlers, so he organized a militia, a

(left) Tobacco plant woodcut.

fighting force made up of citizen volunteers. This shocked Berkeley and the other leaders of the colony, who were more afraid of armed white freemen than of hostile Indians.

Ignoring the governor's concerns, Bacon marched against the Indians, but he and his men killed members of a friendly tribe as well as the Susquehanna who had been hostile to the settlers.

Bacon called his expedition a glorious defense. Governor Berkeley did not agree. He declared Bacon a rebel and charged him with treason, a crime punishable by death.

Bacon's response was to march with five hundred armed men to Jamestown, the capital of the colony. Black men, given guns by whites, joined the march. The elite of the colony were terrified. They saw the rebels as a desperate mob of low, ignorant people attacking their betters. Governor Berkeley fled by ship.

When the rebels reached Jamestown, they burned the settlement to the ground. Berkeley returned with a squadron of the English navy. A naval officer named Captain Grantham offered to negotiate with a group of about four hundred rebels. When Grantham told the rebels that they had been pardoned and freed from slavery, most of them agreed to surrender. Eighty black men and twenty white men refused. Grantham promised that they would be allowed to retreat across the York River in safety.

Grantham had lied. The government forces captured all of the rebels by deceit and force, returned black and white servants to their masters, and hanged several dozen of the rebellion's leaders.

(left) Violence erupted in the Virginia colony in what became known as Bacon's Rebellion, 1676.

Bacon escaped the hangman's noose, because he was already dead. He had fallen to disease on the way to Jamestown.

Historians have called Bacon's Rebellion the largest uprising in any American colony before the American Revolution. It was a class revolution that shook the elite landholders to the core. Five years later, Virginia planters urged the king of England to keep royal soldiers in the colony to "prevent or suppress any Insurrection [uprising]."

The Crossroads

After Bacon's Rebellion, large landowners realized that the social order would always be in danger as long as they relied on white labor. The planters had come to a crossroads.

On one hand, they could open up better economic opportunities to white workers, and give landless freemen the vote. This would ease the discontent of the lower classes of whites, but it would weaken the economic advantages of the elite class, and maybe its political control as well.

On the other hand, the planter class could reorganize society on the basis of both class and race by bringing in more African slaves. Instead of depending on an armed white labor force, the planters could exploit black workers who were not allowed to carry guns because of their race.

The planters made the second choice. After Bacon's Rebellion they turned to African slavery as their main system of labor. From 5 percent of Virginia's population in 1675, blacks increased to 25 percent by 1715, and to more than 40 percent by 1750.

Laws placed ever-stricter limits on slaves' rights. Slaves were forbidden to gather in groups or travel. No black person, free or enslaved, could bear a weapon. Interracial relationships were outlawed, and all children of mixed race, no matter which parent was white or free, became slaves.

To protect the interests of their class in the short term, the elite planters of Virginia had made a choice that would have tragic consequences for centuries.

Jefferson and the Problem of Slavery

When the Virginia planters decided in the late seventeenth century to expand slavery, their choice had long-lasting effects. From that time on, slavery and racial conflict were major forces in shaping the history not just of the American South but also of the United States as a whole.

A hundred years after Bacon's Rebellion, a descendant of the Virginia planter class wrestled with the problem of slavery. Thomas Jefferson was a slave-owner who bought and sold black people. He was capable of punishing his slaves with great cruelty. Yet Jefferson also believed that slavery was immoral.

In a work called *Notes on the State of Virginia*, Jefferson recommended abolition, or the end of slavery, which he thought should happen gradually. In a 1788 letter to a friend he spoke of how he wished "to see an abolition not only of the [African slave] trade but of the condition of slavery." He felt guilty about owning slaves and said more than once that when he had paid off all his debts he would set them free. Unfortunately for Jefferson and especially for his slaves, he remained in debt until his death.

Slavery had to be abolished, Jefferson argued, but the freed blacks would have to be removed from American society. Because sending them all out of the country would be impractical and expensive, the best idea Jefferson could come up with was to take children away from their slave mothers, train them to earn a living, and ship them out of the country as soon as they were old enough—perhaps to the independent black Caribbean nation of Haiti. In time, this would lead to the disappearance of the entire black population. Jefferson's plan, however, was never seriously considered.

Why did Jefferson create a plan for removing freed blacks from American society? Slavery was wrong, in his view, but that did not mean that he considered blacks and whites to be equal. Jefferson could not free himself from his belief that the two races were fundamentally different, and that blacks were inferior. The races, he thought, could not live together in America.

The Ears of the Wolf

What worried Jefferson most deeply about the growing slave population was the danger of race war. White prejudice and black resentment, he feared, would one day explode. Years before Jefferson became the third president of the United States, he wrote in *Notes on the State of Virginia*, "Deep-rooted prejudices entertained by the whites; ten thousand recollections, by the blacks, of the injuries they have sustained . . . will divide us into parties, and produce convulsions which will probably never end but in the extermination of the one or the other race." In Jefferson's nightmare, slaves would seize their freedom with daggers.

By Jefferson's time, it was clear that the planters of the seventeenth century had failed to think about what it would mean to change from white indentured servants to African slaves. But although Jefferson understood the problem of slavery, he believed it was too late to do anything about it. "As it is," he wrote in a letter, "we have the wolf by the ears, and we can neither hold him nor safely let him go. Justice is in one scale, and self-preservation in the other." For years after Jefferson's death, the nation would continue to grip the wolf's ears. The African American population would grow, and remain enslaved, while it hungered for freedom.

A SLAVE'S ORDEAL

AFRICANS CARRIED INTO SLAVERY IN NORTH
America endured the nightmarish crossing of the
Atlantic Ocean, a journey known as the Middle Passage. It was vividly described by Olaudah Equiano,
a slave who gained an education and his freedom.
In an autobiography published in 1789, Equiano
wrote of being captured in Africa, marched to the
coast, loaded into the stinking hold of a slave ship,
and taken across the sea to an unknown fate:

> The first object which saluted my eyes when
> I arrived on the coast was the sea, and a
> slave-ship, which was then riding at anchor,
> and waiting for its cargo. These filled me with
> astonishment, which was soon converted
> into terror. . . . When I was carried on board
> I was immediately handled, and tossed up,
> to see if I were sound, by some of the crew;
> and I was now persuaded that I had got into
> a world of bad spirits, and that they were
> going to kill me. . . . When I looked round the
> ship too, and saw a large furnace or copper

boiling, and a multitude of black people of every description chained together, every one of their countenances expressing dejection and sorrow, I no longer doubted of my fate, and, quite overpowered with horror and anguish, I fell motionless on the deck and fainted. . . . I was soon put down under the decks, and there I received such a salutation in my nostrils as I had never experienced in my life; so that with the loathesomeness of the stench, and crying together, I became so sick and low that I was not able to eat. . . . [After a long voyage, the slaves finally sighted land.] We thought . . . we should be eaten by these ugly men . . . there was much dread and trembling among us, and nothing but bitter cries to be heard all the night from these apprehensions, insomuch that at last the white people got some old slaves from the land to pacify us. They told us we were not to be eaten, but to work. . . .

In recent years, some historians have questioned whether Equiano was born in Africa, as he claimed. A few documents suggest that he may have been born in South Carolina. After Equiano became a freeman he joined the movement to end the slave trade. Even if he fictionalized part of his history in order to show his readers the horrors of the Middle Passage, historians know that those horrors did exist. The pain and terror Equiano describes were felt by millions of African captives.

THE ROAD TO THE RESERVATION

IN 1803 PRESIDENT THOMAS JEFFERSON wrote a letter to Andrew Jackson, a young political leader in Tennessee. He told Jackson that the government should encourage Native American people to sell their forests and become farmers, like the whites.

Three decades later, Andrew Jackson was president. Under his leadership, the government forced thousands of Indians off their land. Farming offered no protection—even Native people who were farmers were removed from land that white Americans desired. Jackson's relationship with the Native Americans, however, had begun long before he became president. His own fortunes were tied to what happened to the Indians.

Jackson Against the Indians

Andrew Jackson moved from North Carolina to

(left, detail) Whites hunting buffalo from a moving train, around 1870.

Nashville, Tennessee, in 1787. In Tennessee he practiced law, opened stores, and became a land speculator—someone who buys a lot of land and hopes to sell it for a profit. For example, Jackson paid $100 for 2,500 acres of land along the Mississippi River and immediately sold half of it for $312. Years later he sold the rest of the land for $5,000. The land had once belonged to the Chickasaw people, but Jackson had negotiated a treaty with these Native Americans and opened it to white settlement.

Jackson also had a triumphant military career in wars against the Indians. With the rank of general he led American troops into battle with the Creek people, whom he called "savage bloodhounds" and "blood thirsty barbarians." When Jackson learned that hostile Creek had killed more than two hundred whites at Fort Mims, near what is now Mobile, Alabama, he vowed revenge.

On March 27, 1814, Jackson took his revenge in the Battle of Horseshoe Bend. At a bend in Alabama's Tallapoosa River, Jackson and his troops surrounded eight hundred Creek and killed most of them, including women and children. Afterward his soldiers made bridle reins out of strips of skin taken from the corpses, and Jackson sent

clothing worn by the dead warriors to the ladies of
Tennessee. He told his troops:

> *These fiends . . . will no longer murder our*
> *women and children, or disturb the quiet of*
> *our borders . . . They have disappeared from*
> *the face of the Earth. In their places a new*
> *generation will arise who will know their*
> *duties better.*

Honored as a hero of the Indian wars, Jackson
was elected president in 1828. He supported the
state governments of Mississippi and Georgia,
which wanted to abolish Indian tribal units and
let whites settle on lands that the tribes had been
farming. The tribes' ownership of those lands had
been guaranteed by treaties with the federal, or
national, government—but the states were breaking the treaties.

As Jackson watched the treaties being broken,
he claimed he was helpless to do anything about it.
This was not true. Authority over the Indians lay
with the federal government, not the states, and in
1832 the US Supreme Court ruled that states had
no power to make laws that affected Indian territories. Jackson simply refused to uphold the court's

decision. Behind the scenes, in fact, he was working to have the Indians removed from their land.

The states' goal in breaking the treaties was to end the authority of the tribal chiefs, turning them into ordinary citizens who must follow the laws of the whites rather than their own laws. The chiefs could then be bullied, bribed, or persuaded to move off their lands, and the rest of the Indians would follow. All Jackson had to do was stay out of the way.

In Jackson's view, Indians could not survive within white society. His solution was to set aside a territory west of the Mississippi River "to be guaranteed to the Indian tribes as long as they shall occupy it . . . as long as the grass grows, or water runs." Jackson advised the Indians to move west. Beyond the borders of white society, they would be free to live in peace under their own governments.

Jackson spoke of himself as a good father, wanting only the best for his "red children." Taking the attitude that his position was both legal and morally right, he uprooted seventy thousand Native Americans from their homes and ordered soldiers to move them west of the Mississippi. The removal of the Indians, like the importing of African slaves to work as plantation laborers, helped turn the American South into a cotton kingdom. The major cotton-growing states—Alabama, Mississippi, and Louisiana—were carved out of Indian Territory.

The Choctaw Become "Wanderers in a Strange Land"

The Choctaw of Mississippi were a farming people long before the arrival of whites. They grew corn, beans, squash, pumpkins, and watermelons, and they shared their food freely with tribe members and with neighboring communities that suffered from crop failures.

By the early nineteenth century, many Choctaw had turned to raising cows and pigs in enclosed farms, in the manner of white farmers. Some Choctaw grew cotton to sell, and some owned black slaves. The government did not treat the farming Choctaw in the same way it treated white planters, however. Farming Choctaw suffered the same fate as the rest of their people.

In 1830 the Mississippi state government ended the legal identity of the Choctaw Nation and its ability to govern itself. This meant that individual Choctaw now had to obey state authority. Nine months later, officials from the federal government met with the Choctaw at Dancing Rabbit Creek to negotiate a treaty that would turn their lands over to the government and remove them to the west.

The Choctaw turned down the offer, saying, "It is the voice of a very large majority of the people here present not to sell the land of their forefathers." Thinking that the meeting was over, many Choctaw left. But the federal officials refused to accept no for an answer. They bluntly told the remaining chiefs that the Choctaw must be removed from Mississippi, or they would feel the weight of state law. If they resisted, they would be destroyed by federal forces. Under this threat, the chiefs finally signed the treaty.

The Treaty of Dancing Rabbit Creek gave more than ten million acres of Choctaw land to the federal government. Not all Choctaw had to migrate to the lands west of the Mississippi River, however. Individuals and families could register with federal agents for a land grant in Mississippi, like any white settler. This made it look as if the program gave Choctaw a fair chance to succeed in white society as individual landowners.

In reality, the Choctaw never had a chance. As soon as an Indian acquired a land grant, a speculator loaned money to the Indian, with the title to the land as insurance for the loan. When the Indian was unable to make enough money to repay the loan, the speculator claimed ownership of the land. In other cases, white settlers simply moved onto Indian land and squatted there, refusing to move. The Indians who had claimed land grants and then lost them had to move west, along with the rest of the Choctaw.

A year after the treaty, thousands of Choctaw began their trek to the Indian Territory across the Mississippi River. On the way, many of them encountered terrible winter storms. French traveler Alexis de Toqueville witnessed the Choctaw crossing the great river and wrote of the conditions they faced:

> *It was then the middle of winter, and the cold was unusually severe; the snow had frozen hard upon the ground, and the river was drifting huge masses of ice. The Indians had their families with them, and they brought in their train [procession] the wounded and the sick, with children newly born and old men upon the verge of death.*

Uprooted, many Choctaw felt bitter and angry. In his "Farewell Letter to the American

People, 1832," Choctaw Chief George W. Harkins explained why his people left their ancestral lands: "We were hedged in by two evils, and we chose that which we thought least." The Choctaw had chosen to "suffer and be free" rather than remain under laws that would not let their voices be heard. But they left unwillingly, because their attachment to their native land was strong. "That cord is now broken," Harkins declared, "and we must go forth as wanderers in a strange land!"

The Cherokee on the Trail of Tears

Like the Choctaw in Mississippi, the Cherokee in Georgia were removed from their lands "legally." The Cherokee faced the same choice: leave or bow to white rule.

Under the leadership of Principal Chief John Ross, the Cherokee refused to abandon their homes and lands. They insisted that the federal government must honor the treaties it had made—treaties that had granted the Cherokee Nation ownership of its territory and the right to govern itself. Their appeals fell on deaf ears in Washington. President Jackson sent an official to negotiate a treaty for Cherokee removal.

Not all Cherokee agreed with Chief Ross that they should resist removal. A minority of them supported the idea of removal, and John Ridge, a leader among this group, signed a treaty saying that the Cherokee would leave their land in exchange for a payment of more than three million dollars.

For the treaty to take effect, it had to be ratified, or agreed to, by the entire tribe. The federal official scheduled a meeting for that purpose, but the Georgia militia prevented the Cherokee newspaper from publishing an announcement of the meeting. The militia also threw Chief Ross in jail. Only a tiny fraction of the Cherokee Nation attended the ratification meeting, and no tribal officers were present. Even some federal officials recognized that the treaty was a fraud. Still, President Jackson and the US Congress said it was legal.

The treaty set loose thousands of white settlers who seized the Cherokee lands and forced many Indians to abandon their homes. When the Cherokee refused to migrate, the federal government ordered the military to remove them by force. General Winfield Scott, with seven thousand troops, rounded up the Cherokee in a violent, cruel process, treating them as prisoners.

The Cherokee were marched west in the dead of the winter of 1838–1839. Like the migration of the Choctaw, the journey of the Cherokee brought dreadful suffering. One of the dispossessed Indians said, "Looks like maybe all be dead before we get to new Indian country, but always we keep marching on." By the time the Cherokee reached the new Indian Territory west of the Mississippi, more than four thousand people—nearly a fourth of this exiled nation—had died on what the tribe still remembers as the Trail of Tears.

"What Shall We Do with the Indians?"

The Plains Indians, who lived west of the Mississippi River, also saw their way of life changed forever by the march of white settlement and civilization. The fate of one Plains tribe, the Pawnee, was similar to that of the Southern Indians.

Traditionally the Pawnee had lived by farming corn and hunting buffalo in central Nebraska and northern Kansas. The buffalo hunt was a sacred activity, and the number of animals killed was strictly limited to what the Pawnee were able to consume. Then, during the nineteenth century, the Pawnee began to take part in the fur trade.

Hunting started to become a commercial activity. Contact with white traders also introduced new diseases like smallpox, which reduced the Pawnee population from ten thousand in 1830 to only four thousand in 1845.

By then, an even greater threat to the Pawnee had emerged. It was the railroad. In his 1831 message to Congress, President Jackson praised science for expanding man's power over nature by linking the cities together with railroads. At that time the United States had just seventy-three miles of railroad track, but the network of railways would grow. Thirty years later in 1860 the United States would have 30,636 miles of track—more than the whole continent of Europe.

The railroad brought a new, modern era, one in which horses and Indians would have no place. "In a few years, like Indians, [horses] will be merely traditional," declared a newspaper editorial in 1853. The railroads crisscrossed the Plains and reached toward the Pacific Coast, bringing the frontier to an end.

Another writer asked in 1867, "What shall we do with the Indians?" His answer was that the Indians must take their place in white society, under white laws, or be "exterminated."

Railroad Politics

Behind the railroads were powerful corporations, deliberately planning the settlement of the West and the growth of their business interests. Railroad companies saw the Native Americans as obstacles. They lobbied the government for rights-of-way that would let them build tracks through what had been set aside as Indian land.

The railroad companies also pushed for passage of a law called the Indian Appropriation Act of March 3, 1871, which said "no Indian nation or tribe within the territory of the United States shall be acknowledged or recognized as an independent nation, tribe, or power, with whom the United States may contract by treaty." As one lawyer for a railroad company pointed out, the Act destroyed the political existence of the tribes. It allowed the companies to build tracks across America, opening the West to new settlement. All this was seen by whites as the progress of civilization.

Indians saw it very differently. They watched the railroad carry white hunters to the Plains, turning the prairies into buffalo killing fields. They found carcasses rotting along the tracks, a trail of death for the animal that had been the main source of life for the Plains Indians. At the same time, white

(left) Whites hunting buffalo from a moving train, around 1870.

settlers complained that the Pawnee occupied some of the best land in the region. Settlers, their newspapers, and their leaders called on Washington to remove the Indians.

The Pawnee also found themselves under attack from the Sioux, a Plains people who had lived to the north. Pushed south by the white settlers moving into their lands and by the decline of the buffalo, the Sioux attacked the Pawnee, burned their crops, and stole their food. In 1873 the Sioux attacked a Pawnee hunting party at what came to be known as Massacre Canyon and killed more than a hundred of them.

Stunned by this tragedy, the Pawnee had to decide whether they should retreat to federal reservations for protection. In spite of the anguish of leaving their homeland, most felt they had no choice. They migrated to a reservation in Kansas.

The identity and existence of the Pawnee had depended on the boundlessness of their sky and earth. But now railroad tracks cut across their land like long gashes, and fences enclosed their grasslands where buffalo once roamed. Indians had become a minority on land they had occupied for thousands of years.

A Pawnee named Overtakes the Enemy said,

"To do what they [whites] called civilizing us . . .
was to destroy us. You know they thought that
changing us, getting rid of our old ways and language and names would make us like white men.
But why should we want to be like them, cheaters
and greedy?" The world the Plains Indians had
known was coming to an end.

A FAMILY'S
TERRIBLE TREK

"LONG TIME WE TRAVEL ON WAY TO NEW LAND,"
a Cherokee said. "People feel bad when they leave
Old Nation. Women cry and make sad wails. Children cry and many men cry, and all look sad when
friends die, but they say nothing, just put heads
down and keep on going towards West."

Four thousand Cherokee, including many children, died of cold, hunger, or disease on the Trail
of Tears in the winter of 1838–1839. Those who
survived would have to make a new life in the unfamiliar land west of the Mississippi River.

Leaders among the Cherokee came forward to
help their people during and after the trek. Jesse
Bushyhead was one of them. His grandfather, John
Stuart, had come to North America from Scotland
with the British army before the American Revolution. Stuart married a Cherokee woman and spent
the rest of his life among her people, who gave him
the name Bushyhead because of his distinctive
mop of red curls.

Jesse Bushyhead, Stuart's grandson, was raised

in the traditional Cherokee culture, but he also attended schools run by white missionaries. By the time the US government began removing the Cherokee from their land, Jesse Bushyhead had become a Baptist minister, a missionary to the Indians, and an interpreter who helped Indians and government officials communicate.

Bushyhead opposed the government's removal of the Cherokee. When he realized that it could not be avoided, he gathered together his family and about a thousand other Cherokee, mostly Christians, and led them west. The journey lasted six months. By the time Bushyhead and his followers reached the Indian Territory in Oklahoma, eighty-two members of the group had died—but this was a better record than many of the bands that traveled the Trail of Tears.

One person lost from Bushyhead's group was his seventeen-year-old daughter, who died soon after the travelers had crossed the Mississippi. Other Bushyhead children survived. They would follow in their father's footsteps by becoming leaders and helpers of the Cherokee people.

In the tribe's new home, Jesse Bushyhead served as an elder of the Baptist church and had the responsibility of distributing food sent by the government to the Indians. His son Dennis left the reservation to attend Princeton University and then to join the California Gold Rush in 1849, but he later returned and took up his role as a chief in Cherokee politics.

One well-known member of the Bushyhead clan was Jesse's daughter Carrie, who was four years old when the family set out on the Trail of Tears. Carrie survived the journey. After the family reached Oklahoma, she attended a school for Cherokee girls, then went on to teach many Cherokee children at another school, the Baptist Mission. Long after her death in 1909, this survivor of the Trail of Tears was remembered by her students and others in the community as Aunt Carrie.

NATIVE AMERICANS LIVED OUTSIDE of white society's borders. African Americans, though, lived among whites. In the South they lived on plantations. In the North they lived in ghettos. One black man who knew both these worlds was David Walker.

Born in North Carolina in 1785, Walker was the son of a slave father and a free mother. He inherited his mother's status and was free. Still, the sight of people who shared his skin color being defined as property filled him with rage against the cruelty and injustice of slavery. Somehow Walker learned to read and write. He studied history and thought about the question of why blacks in America were in such a terrible condition.

Walker continued to reflect on this question after he moved north to Boston, where he sold old clothes. Freedom in Northern society, he realized, was only a pretense. In reality, Northern blacks were treated as inferior, allowed to do only menial jobs such as cleaning white men's shoes.

Slavery, Walker believed, could be destroyed only through violence. In 1829 he published *Appeal to the Coloured Citizens of the World,* in which he said, "Masters want us for their slaves and think nothing of murdering us. . . ." He added that if enslaved blacks ever rose up against their oppressors, it would be "kill or be killed." Lawmakers in the South prevented Walker's book from being widely distributed. In the North, even white abolitionists who opposed slavery criticized its strong language. But what Walker had presented was a disturbing view of the condition of blacks in America. They were slaves in the South and outcasts in the North.

Northern Freedom?

In 1860 there were 225,000 African Americans in the Northern states. They were "free," because the North had abolished slavery after the American Revolution. Still, they were the targets of poisonous racism.

Everywhere blacks experienced discrimination and segregation. They were barred from most hotels and restaurants. In theaters and churches they had to sit in separate sections, always in the back. Black children usually attended separate, inferior schools. Told that their presence in white neighborhoods would lower property values, blacks found themselves trapped in crowded, dirty slums. They were excluded from good jobs—in the 1850s nearly 90 percent of working blacks in New York had menial jobs. "No one will employ me; white boys won't work with me . . ." a young African American man complained.

Blacks were also limited in their right to vote. In New York, for example, a white man could qualify to vote in a number of ways: by owning property, paying taxes, serving in the militia, or working on the highways. A black man was required to own property in order to vote. Pennsylvania went further. In 1838 it limited the vote to white males only.

In addition, African Americans suffered from attacks by whites. Time and again in Northern cities, white mobs invaded black communities, killing people, and destroying their homes and churches. Philadelphia, the "city of brotherly love," was the scene of several bloody riots against blacks. In 1834, for example, whites on the rampage forced blacks to flee the city.

Society's widespread view was that blacks were inferior to whites. Blacks were called childlike, lazy and stupid, or prone to criminal behavior. Interracial relationships were feared as a threat to white racial purity. Indiana and Illinois outlawed interracial marriage, and even where it was legal, it was strongly disapproved of. All in all, for blacks the North was not the Promised Land. They were not slaves, but they were hardly free.

On Southern Plantations

Meanwhile, in the South in 1860, four million African Americans were slaves. They accounted for 35 percent of the total population of the region. The majority of them worked on plantations, large farms with more than twenty slaves.

A slave described the routine of a workday:

> The hands are required to be in the cotton
> field as soon as it is light in the morning, and,
> with the exception of ten or fifteen minutes,
> which is given to them at noon to swallow
> their allowance of cold bacon, they are not
> permitted to be a moment idle until it is too

dark to see, and when the moon is full, they oftentimes labor until the midnight.

To manage their enslaved labor force, masters used various methods of discipline and control. They sometimes used kindness, but they also believed that strict discipline was essential and that they had to make their slaves fear them. Senator James Hammond of South Carolina, who owned more than three hundred slaves, explained, "We have to rely more and more on the power of fear. We are determined to continue Masters, and to do so we have to draw the rein tighter and tighter day by day." Physical punishment was common.

Masters also used psychological control, trying to brainwash slaves into believing that they were racially inferior and suited for bondage. Kept illiterate and ignorant, they were told that they could not take care of themselves.

White Southerners held two contrasting images of the African Americans as slaves. In one view, the slaves were childlike, irresponsible, affectionate, lazy, and happy. Together these qualities made up a personality that came to be called the "Sambo"—the smiling slave who loved his or her master.

The image of the smiling slave had special meaning for slaveholders. The world disapproved of American slavery, which made slaveholders want to prove that it was really a good thing. If owners could show their enslaved workers as happy and satisfied, and that slaves needed the protection of their masters, then perhaps they could defend themselves against those who called slavery immoral.

But there was another, darker view of slaves

throughout the South. In this view, blacks were savages, barbarians who could turn violently against their masters at any moment. Slaveholders were terrified of black revolts and uprisings. One slaveholder in Louisiana recalled times when every master went to bed with a gun at his side.

Slave uprisings did occur. In 1832 in Virginia, an enslaved man named Nat Turner led seventy other slaves in a violent rebellion that lasted two days and left almost sixty whites dead. Turner admitted that he had no reason to complain of the treatment he had received from his master. The revolt, he said, was sparked by a religious vision. He had seen black and white spirits fighting, and a voice told him to rise up against his enemies with their own weapons.

Before the revolt, Turner had seemed humble, obedient, and well behaved. He may have fit the image of "Sambo," the happy slave. For slave owners, viewing their slaves as Sambos comforted their troubled consciences, and also reassured them that their slaves were under control. But slaves who behaved like Sambos might have been acting, playing the role of loyal slaves in order to get favors or to survive, while keeping their inner selves hidden. Nat Turner's rebellion made whites

(left) The "Sambo" figure in this 1899 poster represents a white fantasy of African Americans.

nervous because it showed that even a seemingly "good" slave could be planning their destruction.

African Americans in Southern Cities

Not all slaves lived and worked on plantations. In 1860 there were 70,000 urban slaves in the South, laboring in cloth mills, iron furnaces, and tobacco factories. Many had been "hired out" by their masters to work as wage earners. The masters received weekly payments from the slaves' employers or from the slaves themselves. One slave in Savannah, Georgia, used the hiring-out system to his own advantage. First he bought his own time from his master at $250 a year, paying in monthly installments. Then he hired seven or eight slaves to work for him.

Hiring-out weakened the slave system. No longer under the direct supervision of their masters, slaves could feel the loosening of the reins. They were taking care of themselves and enjoying a taste of independence. By associating with free laborers, both black and white, they learned what it meant to be free. It would take a devastating war, however, to finally cut the reins that bound the enslaved blacks of the South.

Frederick Douglass:
From Slave to Reformer

Frederick Douglass was born into slavery on the Maryland plantation of Thomas Auld around 1818. His mother was a black slave. His father was a white man, possibly Auld. Douglass spent his earliest years in the cabin of his black grandparents, where he was protected from what he later called "the bloody scenes that often occurred on the plantation."

As a young boy, Douglass was placed in the home of Hugh Auld, his master's brother, who lived in Baltimore. At first things went well. Auld's wife, Sophia, seemed like a mother to the young slave. When Douglass developed a strong desire to learn to read, she gave him lessons. The boy learned quickly, and Sophia was proud of his progress—until she told her husband about it.

Hugh Auld angrily banned any more reading lessons, telling Sophia that education would spoil a slave. Her husband's fury had a damaging effect on Sophia, who not only stopped teaching Douglass but also snatched his book away if she happened to catch him reading. Still, he read whenever he could, and he managed to acquire a few books. He even got spelling lessons from white playmates.

The urban slavery of Baltimore was not as strict and punitive as plantation slavery. It was in Baltimore that Douglass saw that not all blacks were slaves. The sight of free blacks filled him with the desire for escape and freedom. When Douglass was sixteen, however, Thomas Auld sent him to work for a poor farmer named Covey, who was known as a slave breaker. Covey's instructions were to break Douglass's spirit and turn him into an obedient slave. Kicked, beaten, and whipped, Douglass refused to break. On the day when he fought back and stood up to the brutal overseer, Douglass felt that he was a freeman in spirit, even though he remained a slave.

Douglass made several attempts to escape to the free states. Finally, in 1838, with the help of friends, he succeeded in making his way by ferry, train, and steamboat to Philadelphia, and from there to the house of an abolitionist, or antislavery activist, in New York. Douglass joined the abolitionist cause. Until his death in 1895 he was a spokesman against slavery and racism. Blacks, Douglass believed, were Americans. He predicted that they would eventually be blended and absorbed into the American people.

The Civil War Brings Freedom

The Civil War was started by the planter class of the South. Although this elite group made up only 5 percent of the Southern white population, it dominated the politics of the region. Defending their right to profit from slavery, the planter class took their states out of the Union in 1861. President Abraham Lincoln, however, refused to let them break up the United States. The result was the long and bitter Civil War between the Union, or Northern states, and the Confederacy, the Southern states that had broken away.

At first Lincoln refused to let the Northern army enlist African Americans as soldiers, partly because he feared that whites would refuse to fight in an army that had black soldiers. Then, in the spring of 1863, the Union faced a manpower shortage and was at risk of losing the war. Lincoln gave his generals permission to enlist black men.

A total of 186,000 blacks served in the Union army. By war's end, a third of them would be dead or missing in action. But without the help of African American soldiers, as Lincoln said, the war would have been lost.

The war not only preserved the United States unbroken, it also abolished slavery. Lincoln's

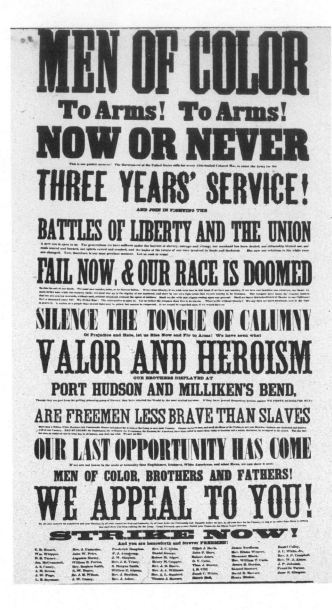

Emancipation Proclamation of 1863 freed the slaves, and the Thirteenth Amendment, ratified to the US Constitution in 1865, ended the institution of slavery.

Although some slaves mourned the deaths of their masters, or worried about how they would live once they were freed, most excitedly embraced their freedom. Thousands of slaves had deserted their masters during the fighting, running off to the Union camps as soon as they heard that Union troops were in the area. White slave-owners were shocked that their faithful "Sambos" would leave them. One woman complained, "They left without even a good-bye."

African Americans in the "New South"

After the Civil War, African Americans were free—but now they had to make their way in a society that had been drastically overturned. The freedmen, as former slaves were called, wanted schools and the right to vote, but most of all they wanted land, so that they could support themselves and their families.

A few leading Northern politicians understood the need to give land to the freed slaves. They

(left) Union army recruitment poster, around 1860.

wanted to break up the estates of Confederate planters and distribute them to the freedmen. Most politicians opposed this idea, however, and it never became law.

During the war, forty thousand blacks had been granted land by a military order from William T. Sherman, a Union general. He set aside large sections of Georgia and South Carolina for black people, who were given titles to forty acres each. Although the titles would not be final until Congress approved the order, the blacks thought they owned the land. But Andrew Johnson, who became president after Lincoln was assassinated, pardoned the Southern planters, who then began to reclaim their former lands and force their former slaves to work for them. When some blacks said they were prepared to defend their acres with guns, federal troops seized the land, tore up the blacks' title papers, and restored the land to the planters.

This ended the possibility of real freedom. As one Union general told Congress, "I believe it is the policy of the majority of farm owners to prevent Negroes from becoming landholders. They desire to keep the Negroes landless, and as nearly in a condition of slavery as it is possible for them to do."

Blacks in the South, no longer slaves but unable to get land of their own, became wage earners or sharecroppers, agricultural laborers who worked the land of their former masters in exchange for a part of the crop. Forced to buy goods from stores owned by the planters, they found themselves in a vicious economic cycle, making barely enough to pay their debts, never enough to buy land.

Meanwhile, a "New South" was emerging. The cotton kingdom was becoming industrialized. New factories and textile mills sprang up. African Americans became an important source of industrial labor, working in sawmills, mining coal, and building railroads. In 1880, 41 percent of the industrial workers in Birmingham, Alabama, were black. Thirty years later, blacks made up 39 percent of all steelworkers in the South.

Yet during the era of Southern rebuilding, known as Reconstruction, African Americans steadily lost freedoms. Discrimination flourished. New state laws across the South—referred to as Jim Crow laws, after a character in minstrel shows—supported segregation by defining the "Negro's place" in trains, theaters, hospitals, and restaurants. These laws were the basis for racial segregation. White politicians found ways

to disqualify blacks from voting. Antiblack violence—including hundreds of lynchings each
year—forced African Americans to be cautious
about seeking their rights. By the end of the nineteenth century, the possibility of real progress for
blacks was sadly remote.

AN ESCAPED SLAVE
SPEAKS HIS MIND

SOME SLAVES SPOKE OF THEIR MASTERS WITH affection and claimed they had never been abused. They might, however, have been playing a role in order to get favors or to survive, while keeping their inner selves hidden. That was true of J. W. Loguen, one of many thousands of slaves who ran away and escaped to the North.

Loguen was born into slavery in Tennessee in 1813. His mother, Cherry, was a slave. His father was a slave owner. As a young man Loguen tried several times to escape slavery. At the age of twenty-one he succeeded and made his way to Canada. In 1860 Loguen received a letter from his former master's wife.

"You know that we reared you as we reared our own children," she wrote, "that you was never abused, and that shortly before you ran away, when your master asked you if you would like to be sold, you said you would not leave him to go with any body." She demanded a thousand dollars from Loguen as repayment for the property he had stolen from her—property that was his body.

Loguen's answering letter included these passionate words:

> *Wretched woman! Be it known to you that I value my freedom, to say nothing of my mother, brothers and sisters, more than your whole body; more, indeed, than my own life; more than all the lives of all the slaveholders and tyrants under Heaven.*
>
> *You say you have offers to buy me, and that you shall sell me if I do not send you $1,000, and in the same breath and almost in the same sentence, you say, "You know we raised you as we did our own children." Woman, did you raise your own children for the market? Did you raise them for the whipping-post? Did you raise them to be drove off in a coffle in chains? Where are my poor bleeding brothers and sisters? Can you tell? Who was it that sent them off into sugar and cotton fields, to be kicked, and cuffed, and whipped, and to groan and die; and where no kin can hear their groans, or attend and sympathize at their dying bed, or follow in their funeral? Wretched woman! Do you say*

you did not do it? Then I reply, your husband did, and you approved the deed—and the very letter you sent shows me that your heart approves it all. Shame on you.

Loguen settled in New York State and made good use of his freedom. He learned to read, opened several schools for black children, and became an abolitionist. In the years before the Civil War, Loguen turned his home in Syracuse, New York, into a stop on the Underground Railroad, the network of shelters for escaped slaves making their way to freedom.

CHAPTER SIX

THE FLIGHT FROM IRELAND

AMERICA'S ETHNIC LANDSCAPE changed in the first part of the nineteenth century. Native Americans, removed from their traditional homelands, were driven onto reservations in the West. African American slavery expanded in the South. At the same time, a great flow of immigrants from Ireland—more than half of them women—reached American shores.

The Irish newcomers struggled to find their place in a society that was hungry for their labor but treated them with scorn. Along the way, Irish Americans sometimes came into competition or conflict with other ethnic minorities, even though they faced some of the same obstacles.

Beef for Britain

The Irish immigrants thought of themselves as exiles who had been forced to flee from a home-

(left, detail)
Young seam-
stresses work on
Irish lace, New
York City, 1912.

land they loved. Time and again, they complained that they were pushed out of their own country by English oppressors. The large-scale emigration from Ireland in the nineteenth century was deeply rooted in a long history of English oppression.

Beginning in the twelfth century, the English conquest of Ireland caused Irish land to be seized and transferred to colonizers from England. By 1700 the Irish owned only 14 percent of Ireland. Farmers had to rent or lease land from English landowners in order to grow food for their families.

Things got worse in the eighteenth century, when the English landlords decided to make their Irish properties more profitable. Beef was in high demand in Britain, so the landlords began to switch from farming to cattle ranching. Farmers' fields were fenced off for use as cattle pastures, and peasants were thrown out of their homes. Eventually 90 percent of the laborers who had once been needed to plant and harvest crops found themselves out of work.

Ireland became a land of "extremely poor" tenants, who lived on other people's land in "dirty Hovels of Mud and Straw, and clothed only in Rags," according to Benjamin Franklin, who visited in 1771. By the 1830s, Ireland was profiting from the sale of its beef, but the common people had been reduced to wretchedness. Families huddled in huts, sharing a single bed of straw while living on a diet of potatoes.

The Great Famine

There was an alternative to the misery of life in Ireland. By the thousands, Irish people were leaving for America. Letters sent to family and friends back home in Ireland told of the wealth and opportunity available in the United States, where there was no tyranny or oppression from landlords. Between 1815 and 1845, a million Irish came to America.

Still, most Irish hated the thought of leaving Ireland, so they endured their hardships at home. They became migrant workers in their own country, leaving their cottages each spring to seek construction or agricultural work, and then returning to their families in the fall with their rent money sewn inside their clothes. Earnings were meager, but they were enough to rent a small plot of land on which to grow potatoes.

Then in 1845 a little-known fungus appeared and changed the course of Irish history. This blight, or disease, attacked potatoes. Forty percent of the crop rotted in the ground that first year.

The deadly blight came back year after year until 1854, destroying the main food source of the Irish peasants. By 1855, a million people had died of starvation and disease in the Great Famine.

For many landlords, the famine was a chance to turn even more of their property into fields for grazing. Peasants who could not pay their rent were turned out of their huts. The landlords kept shipping beef and grain to British markets, while the starving Irish peasants wandered the countryside like "famished and ghastly skeletons" and families ate seaweed in a desperate attempt to stay alive.

In a panic, one and a half million more Irish fled to the United States during the Great Famine. Barely able to scrape together money for their passage, they traveled on crowded ships, crammed together below deck on plywood shelves. Tens of thousands sickened and died during the passage or immediately afterward. Even after the potato blight had retreated, Irish peasants emigrated from their poverty-stricken homeland. Between 1855 and 1900, two million more emigrated to the United States.

An Army of Workers

Pushed from Ireland by famine and hardship, the immigrants were pulled to America by the opportunity for jobs. They provided labor for the grand building projects that were knitting the United States together—its roads, canals, and railroads. Watching these laborers work on the National Road in Pennsylvania, a farmer described them as an "immortal Irish brigade, a thousand strong, with their carts, wheelbarrows, picks, shovels and blasting tools, grading the commons and climbing the mountainside . . . leaving behind them a roadway good enough for an emperor to travel over."

The Irish helped build the Erie Canal and thousands of miles of railways, but they became disposable workers. They had high accident rates because they were often assigned to do the most hazardous jobs. Irish miners in the Pennsylvania coal mines destroyed their lungs breathing black dust. The many deaths of railroad workers gave rise to a saying: An Irishman is buried under every tie.

America turned out to be a nightmare for many Irish immigrants. They complained of being treated like dogs, or worse, "despised & kicked about." A song told of their disappointment:

I got a letter from a relation
Telling me to hasten across the sea,
That gold was to be found in plenty there
And that I'd never have a hard day or a poor
one again

. . . .

Alas, when I landed
I made for the city without delay;
But I never saw gold on the street corners—
Alas, I was a poor aimless person cast adrift.

Against Other Workers

The Irish immigrants found themselves not only exploited as laborers, but also pitted against Chinese and black workers. One clash took place in New England, where Irish workers in the shoe-making industry struggled against low wages. They also opposed the introduction of factory machines that reduced the need for labor.

In order to speak with a united voice, the workers formed a union called the Knights of St. Crispin. The Crispins quickly became the country's largest labor organization, with fifty thousand members by 1870. Demanding higher pay and a workday of only eight hours, the Crispins, in a factory in North Adams, Massachusetts, went on strike, refusing to work until the factory owner agreed to negotiate with them.

Instead, the owner brought in seventy-five Chinese workers from San Francisco to replace the striking Crispins. The Chinese workers were housed in dormitories inside the locked and guarded factory yard. Within three months they were manufacturing more shoes than the same number of white workers had been producing before the strike, which increased profits for the factory owner. Newspapers hailed the owner's move as a success.

The factory owner's action had a sobering effect on workers striking at nearby shoe factories. Ten days after the Chinese workers arrived, the strikers at the other factories, fearful of losing their jobs, went back to work—at a 10 percent pay cut. A magazine suggested that business owners might find Chinese workers to be the solution to the problem of unions and organized labor in the United States. The Chinese were held up as a model for Irish laborers. Chinese workers were said to be harder working and quicker to learn than the Irish.

The Irish immigrant laborers were also believed to be savage and uncivilized, and to lack intelligence

and self-control. In a sermon called "The Dangerous Classes in Society," Reverend Theodore Parker
of Boston claimed that some people were "inferior
in nature." These "lower" beings, he said, were
"Negroes, Indians, Mexicans, Irish, and the like."

In Ireland, people had seen parallels between
their own lives as "slaves" of the British and the
lives of the enslaved and oppressed American
blacks. In 1842, for example, thousands of Irish
citizens signed an antislavery petition that called
blacks their equals and brothers. But when the
Irish crossed the Atlantic, they seemed to lose
their sympathy for African Americans. In America, many of them became antiblack.

As they competed against blacks for jobs, Irish
immigrants called attention to their race. In a
"country of the whites," they asked, shouldn't
white workers be chosen over blacks? Because
many white Protestant Americans despised the
Irish as Catholics and foreigners, Irish newcomers tried to become insiders, to be accepted as
Americans, by showing their fellow whites that
they too were hostile to blacks. Identifying African
Americans as "the other" was a way for the Irish to
assimilate, or blend, into white society.

African Americans reacted to Irish hostility with

their own anti-Irish complaints. They resented being told by the Irish to go back to Africa, a place they had never seen. They claimed that the Irish foreigners took jobs from American-born people. Black journalist John E. Bruce wrote, "It is to be regretted that in [America] where the outcasts— the scum of European society—can come and enjoy the fullest social and political privileges, the Native Born American with wooly hair and dark complexion is made the Victim. . . ."

The Irish had felt the sting of English prejudice and oppression in Ireland. In America they often turned their rage against others on the lower ranks of society's pecking order. Their hostility toward blacks exploded during the Civil War, when Democratic politicians warned that Republicans were willing to sacrifice the lives of Irish soldiers in order to free the slaves, who would then be brought North to "steal the work and the bread of the honest Irish." Fired up by such fears, Irish rioters turned on blacks in New York City in July 1863. Four days of rioting ended only when an army regiment arrived to restore order. More than a hundred people had been killed.

A Massive Migration of Women

Labor competition between Irish and blacks was fierce in the domestic services. In 1830 the majority of the maids, housecleaners, cooks, and other servants in New York City were black. Twenty years later, Irish women filled the majority of domestic service jobs. The daughters of Irish farmers did not just become maids in America, however. They also became factory workers in textile towns such as Lowell, Massachusetts, and Providence, Rhode Island.

More than half of the Irish immigrants were women. (In contrast, women made up just 21 percent of the immigrants from southern Italy and 4 percent of those from Greece.) This massive flight of women from Ireland meant that by 1867, Irish women outnumbered Irish men in New York City: 117,000 to 87,000.

Irish women left their homeland because economic conditions there hit them especially hard. After about 1815 it became common for farmers to leave their land to just one son, rather than dividing it up among their children. Sons who did not inherit land had little choice except to emigrate. This meant that there were fewer men in Ireland who could afford to get married. Young women found their chances of marriage extremely limited, unless their families could afford dowries, money that would go to their husbands' families.

Marriage rates declined. So did the market for goods produced by small, cottage-based manufacturing, such as weaving, which had traditionally been a source of income for women. As a result of these two trends, thousands of women were shut out of Ireland's economy.

Possibilities for both money and marriage, however, waited for Irish girls on the other side of the Atlantic. Women without dowries could find husbands in America. They could also find jobs, especially as maids.

Irish women were more likely to enter domestic service than women of other immigrant groups. In part this was because women of other nationalities often came to America with their husbands or fathers, while many Irish immigrant women were unmarried and unattached to families. As domestic servants, they would receive housing and meals as well as wages.

Service work offered more than shelter, food, and money, however. It was also an introduction to the new culture in which the immigrants found themselves. These young women had come to the United States to settle permanently. Living with their employers helped them adapt to their new society by giving them an inside look at middle-class America.

But while they lived inside American homes, maids were still outsiders. Faraway from their own families, some servants hungered for closeness with the families they served, but often they were ignored. "What I minded . . . was the awful lonesomeness," recalled one former maid. The family members had nothing to do with her, except to give her orders. "It got to feel sort of crushing at last."

The work was demanding, too. Domestic servants cooked, cleaned, cared for children, climbed stairs endlessly, and were expected to be on call around the clock. This lack of personal freedom led one woman to choose factory work over service:

> *It's freedom that we want when the day's work is done. I know some nice girls . . . that make more money and dress better and everything for being in service. . . . But they're never sure of one minute that's their own when they're in the house. Our day [at the factory] is ten hours long, but when it's done it's done, and we can do what we like with the evenings.*

But factory labor was also hard to endure. The

textile mills of New England, where Irish women were a large part of the workforce, were dusty and noisy. Working conditions were dangerous. In 1860, for example, a mill in Lowell collapsed, trapping nine hundred workers. A fire broke out, adding to the terror and devastation. Eighty-eight people died.

Irish women were heavily employed in the sewing trades. "No female that can handle a needle need be idle," one of them wrote home. By 1900 a third of all seamstresses and dressmakers in the United States were Irish women. Like jobs in the textile factories, though, sewing work was often exhausting, dirty, and repetitive.

Still, for many Irish women, America really was a land of opportunity. A daughter wrote home to her father in 1850 to say "this is a good place and a good country." America represented not only jobs and wages but also self-sufficiency, a chance for women to take care of themselves without depending on husbands or fathers. As one of them wrote to a younger sister still in Ireland, "I am getting along splendid and likes my work . . . it seems like a new life."

Irish Power

Irish immigrant women were mainly limited to

domestic service or factory work, but their daughters had more choices. In 1900, 61 percent of Irish women who had immigrated were seamstresses or laundresses, but only 19 percent of the Irish women who had been born in America followed those trades. Irish American daughters were getting educations and entering white-collar jobs such as teaching, nursing, and secretarial work.

Advances for Irish women reflected a broader pattern of Irish success, as the second genera-

tion moved up the social and economic ladder. The family of John Kearney of Poughkeepsie, New York, is an example of that pattern. Kearney emigrated from Ireland to America, where he worked first as an unskilled laborer and then as a junk dealer. One of his sons rose from postal clerk to superintendent of city streets, and another started as a grocery clerk and eventually became the inspector of the city's waterworks.

The fact that the Irish were white helped them assimilate into the mainstream. White immigrants could become naturalized citizens. White young people could apply to the best colleges and universities. The Chinese were prevented by racial laws from becoming naturalized citizens, and large numbers of African Americans had had their right to vote stripped away. But Irish Americans had suffrage, and they used their right to vote to gain political power.

In urban areas with large Irish populations, including New York, Philadelphia, and Boston, Irish voters supported Irish candidates. By 1890 the Irish had captured most of the Democratic Party organizations in Northern cities. Mayors and city councilmen, in turn, rewarded voters with jobs in police and fire departments, city-owned subways and ports, and in city hall itself. Irish

(left) Young seamstresses work on Irish lace, New York City, 1912.

political bosses also awarded public works projects to Irish-owned construction companies. At the same time, ethnic associations for people of Irish descent served as job networks, in which people helped each other find work. Through these ethnic strategies, Irish Americans cooperated with each other to rise from rags to riches.

At the same time, though, the success of the Irish Americans challenged their sense of ethnic identity and unity. Some immigrants urged each other to teach their children Gaelic, the Irish language. They wanted Irish Americans to keep alive their connection to Ireland and its history. Other Irish Americans, however, celebrated the fact that life in the United States was different from the old life. One immigrant said:

> *The second generation here are not interested in their ancestors . . . we have never told them of the realities of life [in Ireland], and would not encourage any of them to visit. When we left there, we left the old world behind, we are all American citizens and proud of it.*

LEADS A CHILDREN'S CRUSADE

MARY HARRIS WAS ONE OF SEVERAL MILLION Irish girls who emigrated to the United States. Later in life, when she was known as Mother Jones, she fought for the rights of American workers, including children. Her activism on behalf of the working class led one lawyer to call her "the most dangerous woman in America."

Mary was born in the Irish city of Cork in 1837. When she was fourteen or fifteen her family left Ireland for Canada, then later moved to the United States. Mary became a schoolteacher and dressmaker. She married George Jones, the organizer of a labor union for ironworkers.

After Mary Harris Jones lost her husband and their four children to disease, and lost her home and dress shop in the Great Chicago Fire of 1871, she got involved in the labor movement that was sweeping the nation, as working people fought for safer job conditions and better pay. She organized support for labor unions and helped lead workers' strikes. Recognizing that labor struggles affected whole families, she got the strikers' wives and children to march in public displays of support for the union cause.

At the beginning of the twentieth century it was still legal to employ children in mines and mills. Some children worked for up to sixty hours a week, for low wages. Bitterly opposed to this exploitation, in 1903 Jones organized a march of about two hundred people, many of them child workers. Over several weeks they marched from Philadelphia, Pennsylvania, to the home of President Theodore Roosevelt in Oyster Bay, New York. The young people carried banners with slogans such as "We Want to Go to School, Not to the Mines!"

In speeches along the way, Jones called for stricter laws governing child labor. The speech she delivered to a crowd in Coney Island is known as "The Wail of the Children." It begins:

> *After a long and weary march, with more miles to travel, we are on our way to see President Roosevelt at Oyster Bay. We will ask him to recommend the passage of a bill by Congress to protect children against the greed of the manufacturer. We want him to hear the wail of the children, who never have a chance to go to school, but work from ten to eleven hours a day in the textile mills of Philadelphia,*

weaving the carpets that he and you walk on, and the curtains and clothes of the people.

Fifty years ago there was a cry against slavery, and the men of the North gave up their lives to stop the selling of black children on the block. To-day the white child is sold for $2 a week, and even by his parents, to the manufacturer. . . .

We will ask in the name of the aching hearts of these little ones that they be emancipated. I will tell the President that I saw men in Madison Square last night sleeping on the benches and that the country can have no greatness while one unfortunate lies out at night without a bed to sleep on. I will tell him that the prosperity he boasts of is the prosperity of the rich wrung from the poor.

In Georgia where children work day and night in the cotton mills they have just passed a bill to protect song birds. What about the little children from whom all song is gone? . . .

You are told that every American-born male citizen has a chance of being President. I tell you that the hungry man without a bed in the park would sell his chance for a good square meal, and these little toilers, deformed,

*dwarfed in body, soul, and morality, with
nothing but toil before them and no chance
for schooling, don't even have the dream that
they might someday have a chance at the
Presidential chair.*

The Children's Crusade, as Mother Jones's
march was called, failed to achieve its goal of a
meeting with the president, but it drew public
attention to the issue of putting children to work.
Historians of the labor movement in America
call the Children's Crusade, led by an immigrant
woman from Ireland, an important early step
toward better child labor laws.

CHAPTER SEVEN

THE WAR AGAINST MEXICO

WHILE IRISH WOMEN WORKED in the textile mills of Massachusetts and Irish men built roads and railway tracks, America's frontier moved westward. The United States grew larger by acquiring territory from other nations by purchase, treaty, or force. In the 1840s, the Mexican-American war gave Irish immigrant men another job to do for the United States—serving as soldiers in a conflict with the neighboring nation of Mexico. That war greatly enlarged the American empire by adding California and the Southwest to the United States. It also added another ethnic group to American diversity: Mexicans.

The Troubled Region Called Tejas

The first conflicts between the United States and Mexico took place in a Mexican territory called

Tejas—or, as it is known today, Texas. Although Texas was part of Mexico, Americans began crossing the Mexican border to settle there in the 1820s. Many were slaveholders from the South in search of new lands on which to grow cotton.

In 1826 President John Quincy Adams tried to buy Texas for a million dollars, but Mexico refused. A year later, worried about US expansion westward, the Mexican government investigated the situation in Texas. It found a growing number of Americans living there, breaking Mexican laws, and taking possession of land without permission from the authorities. When visiting the American settlement at Austin, a Mexican lieutenant, José Maria Sánchez, predicted, "In my judgment, the spark that will start the conflagration that will deprive of us Texas will start from this colony."

To stem the tide of Americans, in 1830 the Mexican government outlawed slavery and banned any more American immigration into Texas. American foreigners in Texas were furious. Many were determined to defy Mexico's antislavery law. At the same time, more Americans crossed the border into Mexico as illegal aliens. By 1835 there were twenty thousand Americans in Texas, greatly outnumbering the four thousand Mexicans.

Tensions grew. Stephen Austin, an American colonizer who had brought three hundred families of settlers into Texas in the 1820s with the permission of the Mexican government, now urged his countrymen to "Americanize" Texas and bring the territory under the US flag. He called for Americans to come to Texas, bringing rifles with them, for conflict between the civilized white Americans and the "mongrel Spanish-Indian and negro race" of Mexico, he believed, was unavoidable. "War is our only recourse," he declared. "There is no other remedy."

War Breaks Out

War came in 1836 when some Americans in Texas began an armed uprising by barricading themselves inside a fort called the Alamo in the town of San Antonio. The Mexican government declared their action illegal and sent troops to end the rebellion. The rebels refused to surrender. Most were killed in the battle that followed. The Mexican army then captured the nearby town of Goliad and executed four hundred American prisoners there.

Under the rallying cry "Remember the Alamo!" the Americans counterattacked, killing 630 Mexican soldiers and capturing their leader. The victorious Americans declared Texas an independent country and named it the Lone Star Republic.

The new republic—which Mexico refused to recognize—did not remain independent for long. In 1845 it was annexed, or added, to the United States. Mexico broke off diplomatic relations with the United States in protest. Tensions between the two countries then focused on a border dispute that involved two rivers.

The United States claimed that the border between Texas and Mexico was the Rio Grande. Mexico insisted that the border was 150 miles to the north, at the Nueces River. Both countries sent troops into the territory between the two rivers. US forces under General Zachary Taylor blockaded the mouth of the Rio Grande, preventing Mexican boats and ships from entering it—an act of war according to international law.

In May 1846 an armed skirmish between troops from both sides gave the US government the excuse it needed to declare war on Mexico. President James Polk said, "War exists notwithstanding all our efforts to avoid it." In reality, the border dispute hid the real reason behind the war. That reason was California.

The Taking of California

California had been colonized by Spain, which regarded California as part of its Mexican colony and began sending settlers there in 1769. Although some of the settlers were of Spanish blood, many were desperately poor people of mixed Indian and black blood who came to California from Mexico. In exchange for moving to the remote and wild California territory, settlers of Spanish blood received land grants and herds of cattle, while the poorest settlers became laborers. The total number of settlers remained small.

Mexico—including California—gained its independence from Spain in 1821. At the time there were only about three thousand Spanish and Mexicans living in California. A few Anglos, or people from the United States, also lived there. The Anglos were generally accepted. The Mexican government even offered them land grants if they converted to Catholicism and became naturalized citizens of Mexico.

By the 1840s more Anglo settlers were entering California, but now they came as illegal aliens because Mexico had outlawed further immigration. War between the United States and Mexico was looming on the horizon, and a key goal of the US government was to gain ownership of California. The territory was an important source of raw materials, such as the cattle hides that were made into boots and shoes in the factories of New England.

Even more important, California was at the edge of North America, on the Pacific Ocean. Its coast had several good harbors, and American whaling ships and naval ships in the Pacific needed harbors where they could make repairs and get supplies. The nation's policymakers also wanted to promote American trade across the Pacific. In a speech to Congress, President Polk spoke of how California's harbors would shelter American ships and would quickly become centers of "an extensive and profitable commerce with China, and other countries of the East."

In California, the war between the United States and Mexico began in the small town of Sonoma when a band of armed frontiersmen invaded the home of the Mexican general who was in charge of the territory north of San Francisco. These rebels raised a flag with the image of a bear and declared that California was now the independent Bear Flag Republic. Soon afterward, a US naval commander sailed his ship into Monterey Bay and claimed California for the United States.

American Conquest

The taking of California turned out to be almost nonviolent. In the Southwest, however, the war had unleashed a brutal military campaign. When US military forces marched into Mexico, they were accompanied by a horde of American volunteers who fought alongside the soldiers. American forces committed many acts of violence against Mexican civilians, ordinary people not involved in the fighting.

One report of these acts came from a young captain named Ulysses S. Grant, who would later become president of the United States. "Since we have been in Matamoros a great many murders have been committed," Grant wrote. "Some of the volunteers and about all the Texans seem to think it perfectly right to impose on the people of a conquered city to any extent, and even to murder them where the act can be covered by dark. And how much they seem to enjoy acts of violence too!"

General Winfield Scott, the commander of the American army in Mexico, admitted that American soldiers had "committed atrocities to make Heaven weep and every American of Christian morals blush for his country. Murder, robbery and rape of mothers and daughters in the presence of tied-up males of the families have been common all along the Rio Grande."

The horror ended in early 1848, a few months after Scott's army occupied the capital, Mexico City. In the Treaty of Guadalupe Hidalgo, Mexico accepted the Rio Grande as the border of Texas. Mexico also turned the Southwest territories over to the United States in exchange for $15 million. The treaty gave the United States a vast new territory: New Mexico, Arizona, Nevada, parts of Colorado and Utah, and California, its prime target. Together with Texas, these territories had made up more than half of Mexico.

"Foreigners in their Own Land"

Many Americans saw the war and conquest as glorious, the triumph of a superior people over an inferior one. Some even believed that God intended Americans to populate and civilize the entire continent. Newspaper editor and poet Walt Whitman wrote, "What has miserable, inefficient Mexico . . . to do with the great mission of peopling the New World with a noble race?"

Mexicans had a different view of the Anglo conquest. Their national border had been moved,

and suddenly thousands of Mexicans found themselves inside the United States. Under the Treaty
of Guadalupe Hidalgo, Mexicans in the new US
territories could either move south across the new
border into Mexico, or stay in the United States. If
they stayed, they would be guaranteed the rights of
American citizens.

Most stayed, not wanting to uproot their
families and leave their homes and land. Yet as
more and more Anglos streamed into the former
Mexican territories, the Mexicans living there felt
like strangers, surrounded by people who spoke
only English. A Mexican diplomat named Manuel
Crescion Rejon said, "Descendants of the Indians
that we are, the North Americans hate us . . . and
they consider us unworthy to form with them one
nation and one society." A few years later, a man
named Pablo de la Guerra told the California state
senate that he and the other "conquered" Mexicans
had become "foreigners in their own land."

Anglo over Mexican

Mexicans living in the United States lacked political
power, even though they had been granted suffrage,
or the right to vote. In California, for example, Mexi-

cans originally outnumbered Anglos by ten to one, but they quickly became a minority. The California Gold Rush, which began in 1848, started a massive migration of Anglos into the territory. A year later California had a hundred thousand Anglos and only thirteen thousand Mexicans.

Anglos dominated California's legislature and passed laws aimed at Mexicans. In 1850, for example, the legislature created a tax on foreign miners. In reality it was a tax on Mexican miners, because the tax collectors took fees mainly from Spanish-speaking miners—including US citizens of Mexican ancestry. California's goldfields simmered with ethnic conflict. Anglo miners resented the Mexicans as competitors and made no distinction between citizens of Mexico and Mexican Americans. Mobs of Anglo miners, armed with pistols, knives, pickaxes, and shovels, drove Mexicans away from the gold diggings.

In Texas, Anglos took measures to limit the political participation of Mexicans. During the 1890s, many counties excluded both Mexicans and blacks from primary elections. The state legislature passed other measures, such as a poll tax, that were designed to prevent Mexicans from voting.

Political limitations made it hard for Mexicans not only to vote but also to protect their rights as landowners. The original version of the Treaty of Guadalupe Hidalgo guaranteed that Mexicans who remained in the United States would keep all legal titles to property. The United States Senate, however, removed that part of the treaty. Instead, it said that Mexicans could appeal to American courts to have their land titles confirmed.

But whether the courts would really confirm those titles was another matter. Starting in 1891, claims in New Mexico were decided by a Court of Private Land Claims. Dominated by Anglos, the court confirmed the titles of about two million acres but turned down claims for more than thirty-three million acres. As a result, Anglos wound up owning about four-fifths of the Mexicans' land. In California, many Mexicans lost their claims because the boundaries of their land grants had not been drawn by surveyors with instruments according to American rules. Others lost their land to squatters, Anglos who settled on Mexican-owned property and refused to leave.

Unfamiliar with American law and lacking skill

in speaking English, Mexicans fell prey to Anglo lawyers. If they won their claims, the landowners might have to pay the lawyer as much as a quarter of their land. Others borrowed money at high rates of interest to pay their lawyers. Even landowners who won their claims often had to sell their land to pay off their debts. In the end, many of the Mexican cattle ranchers lost their lands.

Even the climate worked against the Mexican ranchers and farmers. In times of drought, Anglos could protect their land better than Mexicans, because Anglos had better access to bank credit. They could borrow the money to dig deeper wells. After the drought, the Anglos were financially stronger and could buy land from Mexicans who had suffered economic losses during the drought.

One Mexican old-timer in Santa Barbara later described the decline of the Mexican ranchers who had fallen into debt to Anglo merchants and lost their lands. "The Spanish people had to live," he said, "and as the dwindling herds would not pay their bills, they mortgaged their land to the Americanos. They got much of our lands."

From Landholders to Laborers

In 1910 a Mexican American newspaper in Laredo, Texas, reported that "Mexicans have sold the great share of their landholdings and some work as day laborers on what once belonged to them." In Texas as well as in other parts of the United States that had once belonged to Mexico, most Mexicans were no longer landholders. They had become laborers.

Mexicans were extensively used in ranching and agriculture. Mexican vaqueros, or cowboys, taught Anglo cowboys and ranchers their techniques of roping, branding, and handling cattle. But when railway lines brought the era of the long cattle drives to an end, the Mexican cowboys began to vanish. Some of them turned to fieldwork.

Mexican farm laborers had been in the cotton fields since before Texan independence. As cotton growing increased after the Civil War, Mexicans became the mainstay of agricultural labor. They dug irrigation ditches to bring water from rivers and streams to parched areas. Some of their techniques had been brought to the Southwest by the Spanish. Other techniques came from the Pueblo Indians, who had created complex irrigation systems long before the Spanish arrived.

Mexicans also served as an important workforce

in railroad building. During the 1880s a majority of workers on the Texas and Mexican Railroad were Mexican. By 1900 the Southern Pacific Railroad had 4,500 Mexican employees in California. Railroad work was migratory. The workers and their families lived in boxcars and were taken to where they were needed. Mexicans also worked in the mining industries.

Whatever kind of work they did, Mexican laborers found themselves in a system in which job rank was tied to race. On Anglo-owned ranches, for example, managers and foremen were Anglo. Cowhands were Mexican. In the mines, Anglo workers ran machines while Mexicans did the hard and dangerous hand labor.

Even where Mexicans did the same work as Anglos, they were paid less. For example, a congressional investigation found that wage differences in the copper mines of the West were due to systematic discrimination against Mexicans. To justify this race-based system, a mine owner named Sylvester Mowry used language that might have come from a plantation slave owner, saying that "the lower class of Mexicans . . . are docile, faithful, good servants. . . . They have been 'peons' for generations. They will always remain so, as it is their natural condition."

(*left*) Frederick Remington, *A Vaquero*, 1881–1901.

Mexican Workers Get Organized

Like the enslaved blacks of the Old South, Mexican workers showed that they could defy the image of the quiet, obedient servant. Demanding respect and better wages, they repeatedly went on strike. Through strikes, Mexican construction and mine workers succeeded in protecting their jobs as well as gaining higher pay and eight-hour workdays.

Protesting wage cuts in 1903, Mexican and Japanese farm laborers went on strike together in Oxnard, California. They formed a union called the Japanese Mexican Labor Association (JMLA) and held meetings in both Japanese and Spanish, with English as a common language for both groups. For the first time in California history, two minority groups, united by their economic class, had come together to form a union.

The JMLA asked to be included in the American Federation of Labor (AFL), a national organization. The president of the AFL agreed to accept the Mexicans—but not any Japanese or Chinese members.

The Mexican members of the JMLA refused the AFL's terms. The secretary of the Mexican branch of the JMLA wrote, "We beg to say in reply that our Japanese brothers here were the first to recognize the importance of cooperating and uniting in demanding a fair wage scale. . . . We will refuse any other kind of charter, except one which will wipe out race prejudice and recognize our fellow workers as being as good as ourselves."

Without the support of the AFL, the JMLA passed out of existence a few years later, but its strike had shown that Mexican laborers were ready to stand in solidarity with laborers from other ethnic groups.

The most powerful Mexican workers' show of force happened in Arizona. It started in 1903, when 3,500 miners—80 percent of them Mexican—went on strike for equal wages, an eight-hour workday, free hospitalization, and other benefits. The strikers shut down the mines but they had to return to work after heavy rains and flooding destroyed many of their homes. Several strike leaders went to prison, convicted of inciting a riot.

Twelve years later, however, five thousand miners struck again. This time the mine owners sealed the entrances to the mines and told the workers to "go back to Mexico." Hundreds of strikers were arrested during the nineteen-week conflict, but in the end the workers managed to win wage increases.

The strikes brought out a feeling of ethnic solidarity. Mexican musicians entertained the strikers,
and Mexican merchants provided them with food
and clothing. More important, the strikes were
often supported by associations called mutualistas,
which were self-help organizations formed within
the Mexican American community. Members of
the community contributed to the *mutualistas* and
also turned to them for loans, money for hospital
and funeral expenses, and other needs.

As the mutualistas grew and became more
organized, they blew away the myth of Mexicans
as a quiet, siesta-loving, sombrero-wearing people.
Through these ethnic organizations, Mexican
Americans unified to resist racism and exploitation. The mutualistas reflected a dynamic Mexican
American identity—a proud attachment to the
culture south of the border as well as a fierce determination to claim their rights and dignity north of
the border.

BEARS AGAINST VALLEJO

THE US CONQUEST OF CALIFORNIA BEGAN IN
the small town of Sonoma, north of San Francisco.
There, in the early morning of June 6, 1846, General
Mariano G. Vallejo was rudely awakened in his home
by thirty armed Americans. The Americans' home-
made flag displayed the image of a grizzly bear—the
symbol of their Bear Flag Republic. To the Mexicans,
the grizzly was a thief, a stealer of their cattle. They
called the armed intruders *Los Osos*, "the bears."

Vallejo represented Mexican authority, and even
though he was no longer on active duty, the Americans had come to "arrest" him and carry him to
Sacramento as their prisoner. They entered his home,
with its handsome mahogany chairs, fine piano, and
large library. Vallejo offered them wine before he went
to his room to change clothes for the journey.

Unlike his captors, Vallejo had been born in California. He belonged to the elite, educated class and
owned a vast estate, where he lived with his wife, the
mother of sixteen children. Vallejo's brother, sister,
and Anglo brother-in-law also lived nearby. Los Osos
took Vallejo's brother and brother-in-law prisoner, too.

Two months later Vallejo was freed and allowed to
return home. He wrote to a friend that more than a

thousand cattle, six hundred horses, and many other valuable possessions had been stolen in his absence. Later, after California came firmly under US rule, Vallejo fought to keep his land. He lost the title to one land claim in court. He battled all the way to the US Supreme Court to keep the other claim, near Petaluma. Although Vallejo won the legal battle, squatters had settled on his land and refused to move. They also drove away his laborers and burned his crops.

Vallejo was forced to sell off pieces of his land. His estate, which had once covered more than 100,000 acres, shrank to 280 acres. Bitter over the loss of the land, he cursed the new order: "The language now spoken in our country, the laws which govern us, the faces we encounter daily are those of the master of the land, and of course antagonistic to our interests and rights, but what does that matter to the conqueror? He wishes his own well-being and not ours!"

While fighting for his land, Vallejo also took part in the politics of the new state. He was elected to the California legislature in 1850. That same year, he donated land to be used for the new state capital, although the land proved unsuitable and the capital was built elsewhere.

CHAPTER EIGHT

FROM CHINA TO GOLD MOUNTAIN

THE ADDITION OF CALIFORNIA to the United States made it easier for Americans to conduct business with Asia across the Pacific Ocean. It also opened the way to emigration from Asia, as people from China began crossing the Pacific to Californian ports, especially San Francisco.

In 1848, soon after the United States acquired California in the Treaty of Guadalupe Hidalgo, a policymaker named Aaron H. Palmer sent a plan to Congress. Palmer predicted that San Francisco would become a booming hub of commerce. He also recommended that the United States import Chinese workers to build the transcontinental railroad and to farm the fertile lands of California.

Pioneers from Asia

A year after Palmer proposed his plan, Chinese migrants began arriving in America, but they came for their own reasons. China was torn by war, rebellion, high taxes, floods, and famine. These harsh conditions drove many Chinese people to seek survival in America.

At the same time, America seemed to beckon. Hearing about the Gold Rush, Chinese gave California the nickname *Gam Saan,* or Gold Mountain, the land across the sea. Many of the younger, more impatient, and more daring Chinese men left their homes to seek their fortunes. America promised not only gold but also opportunities for employment. In the 1860s a laborer in China could earn three to five dollars a month. In California he could work for the railroad and make thirty dollars a month.

The Chinese migrants were mostly men, planning to work abroad temporarily. They were illiterate, or had little education, but they dreamed of new possibilities. Their goal was to earn money in America and return to China, prosperous and successful. As they prepared to leave their farms and villages, they said goodbye to their wives and families, knowing they would not see them again for years. But they promised to return someday.

And so they left China, by the hundreds and thousands. By 1870 there were 63,000 Chinese in the United States. More than three-fourths of them were in California, but they lived elsewhere in the West, the South, and New England. The

(left) Chinese and European workers building the transcontinental railroad, 1869.

Chinese made up a sizeable share of the population in some places: 29 percent in Idaho, 10 percent in Montana, and 9 percent in California.

By 1930 about four hundred thousand Chinese had made the Pacific crossing. About half of these immigrants stayed in America and made the United States their new home. They could not hope to become US citizens, however. A law called the 1790 Naturalization Act said that only white immigrants could become naturalized citizens.

Working in America

At first California seemed to welcome the Chinese, but as their numbers increased, the political tide began to turn against them. From the goldfields came the cry, "California for Americans!" In 1852 the California legislature answered that cry by passing another miner's tax. Every foreign miner who did not intend to become a US citizen had to pay three dollars a month, which was a significant amount at the time. The tax was aimed primarily at Chinese miners, who were prevented by law from becoming citizens. They were trapped in a state of being foreigners forever.

During the 1860s, two-thirds of the Chinese in

America worked in the California goldfields. Most were independent prospectors, but sometimes they organized into small groups and formed their own companies. Clothed in blue cotton shirts, baggy pants, and wide-brimmed hats, the Chinese miners were a common sight in the California foothills. By 1870 California had collected a total of five million tax dollars from the Chinese immigrants—between a quarter and half of the state's entire income.

Then mining profits started to fall, and the Chinese began leaving the goldfields. Thousands of them, along with newly arrived immigrants, went to work on the railroads. The building of the Central Pacific Railroad, the western part of the first rail line across the entire country, was a Chinese achievement. Chinese workers laid tracks, operated power drills, and handled the explosives needed to blast tunnels through Donner Summit. During the winter of 1866 they lived and worked in tunnels under sixty-foot snowdrifts.

Chinese railroad laborers worked for lower wages than whites. When the white laborers demanded that Central Pacific stop hiring the Chinese, superintendent Charles Crocker told them that if they could not get along with the

Chinese, he would have only one alternative: to fire the whites and hire more Chinese. When the Chinese workers went on strike and asked for the same wages as whites, Crocker isolated the strikers in the mountains and cut off their food supply. After a week the starving workers were back on the job.

After the completion of the Central Pacific Railroad in 1869, thousands of the Chinese workers went to San Francisco, where many of their fellow immigrants were living. The industrialization of San Francisco developed hand-in-hand with the growth of the city's Chinese community. In 1860 San Francisco had just over 2,700 Chinese residents. Ten years later, it had more than 12,000, a quarter of California's Chinese population. Half the labor force in four of San Francisco's key industries—boots and shoes, woolens, cigars and tobacco, and sewing—was Chinese.

Meanwhile, in rural regions the Chinese were contributing to the agricultural industry of California, helping the state to shift from farming wheat to growing fruit. Some Chinese agriculture workers became tenant farmers, working on white-owned land in exchange for half the proceeds from selling the crop. These workers had been experienced farmers in China. They shared their knowledge, teaching their employers how to plant, cultivate, and harvest the crops of orchards and fields. They also shared their skills and techniques in building dams and irrigation systems, turning swamplands into fertile fields. By 1880 more than two-thirds of the farm workers in Sacramento, Solano, and Yuba counties were Chinese.

Targets of Resentment

Chinese workers became targets of white labor resentment, especially during hard times.

"White men and women who desire to earn a living," reported the *Los Angeles Times* in 1893, "have for some time been entering quiet protests against vineyardists and packers employing Chinese in preference to whites." Those protests soon became violent. Economic depression led to brutal anti-Chinese riots by unemployed white workers throughout California. Immigrants from China were beaten, shot, and loaded onto trains and shipped out of town.

Ethnic hostility in the mines, factories, and fields forced thousands of Chinese into self-employment. They opened stores, restaurants, and especially laundries. Many chose laundry work because it was easier and less expensive to open a laundry than to start other businesses. A Chinese laundryman needed only a stove for heating water, a trough for washing, space for drying things, a place to sleep, and a sign. Laundrymen did not even need to speak much English to carry on their business.

But Chinese laundrymen were also pushed into this occupation. Laundry work was not a traditional man's occupation in China, but in America it was one of the few opportunities available to them. The laundry represented a retreat from a labor market that offered limited possibilities.

As Chinese immigrants struggled to earn a living, Americans debated what role the Chinese should play in their society. One view was that the Chinese should remain a permanent class of foreign laborers, working under the direction of white foremen and directors. This idea was rooted in the racist notion that "American" meant "white."

Not all Americans were comfortable with the idea of a large, permanent class of Chinese laborers. Many of the negative ideas and images that had been associated with African Americans and Native Americans were applied to the Chinese, too. The Chinese were called savage, childlike, immoral, and pagan. All three groups shared a common identity: they were people of color. This was made clear in 1854 when California's state supreme court ruled that "Chinese and other people not white" could not give evidence against whites in court. California also passed a state law banning marriage between a white person and an Asian, black, or mixed-race person.

In 1879 President Rutherford B. Hayes issued a racist warning to the American people about the "Chinese problem." He said, "Our experience in dealing with the weaker races—the Negroes and Indians—is not encouraging. I would consider with favor any suitable measures to discourage the Chinese from coming to our shores."

Banned by Law

Three years after Hayes's warning, Congress passed a law called the Chinese Exclusion Act. It prevented Chinese laborers from entering the United States for the next ten years, and it specifically stated that the Chinese who were already in the country could not become citizens. At that time the Chinese made up just 0.002 percent of the US population, but the fears and forces behind the Exclusion Act had little to do with numbers. Chinese men were seen as threats to racial purity.

Something had gone wrong in America, and an age of economic opportunity seemed to be coming to an end. The economy took a downturn. Unemployment rose as thousands of men and women were thrown out of work. In this context of economic crisis and social strife, the Chinese were seen as outsiders who came to "steal" the jobs of white Americans. Support for the Exclusion Act was overwhelming. The law was renewed in 1892, and in 1902 it was extended indefinitely into the future.

Meanwhile, the Chinese fought discrimination. Time and time again they took their struggle for civil rights to the courts. Although the Chinese failed to gain the right to citizenship, Chinese merchants succeeded in winning some protections under the 1870 Civil Rights Act, which guaranteed people of color the same rights as white people to make contracts, give evidence, and be protected by law. They also overturned the Foreign Miner's Tax.

But guarantees of equal protection by federal law had little effect on what happened in society. The Chinese continued to be victims of racial violence. "The Chinese were in a pitiable state in those days," recalled Kin Huie, describing life in San Francisco's Chinatown in the 1870s. "We were simply terrified; we kept indoors after dark for fear of being shot in the back. Children spit upon us as we passed by and called us rats."

Chinese Women in America

Although the great majority of Chinese immigrants were men, a few Chinese women did come to "Gold Mountain." In 1852 there were about tweleve thousand Chinese in California. Seven of them were women. By 1900 about 5 percent of the nation's ninety thousand Chinese were women.

Chinese tradition and culture limited the possibilities of migration for women, who were expected to be obedient to fathers, husbands, and sons. Women were also left behind because it would have been expensive to bring them, and because the men thought they would be gone only temporarily. In addition, conditions in America—including harsh frontier life, hard work, and racial hostility—discouraged women from joining their husbands. In the view of many white Americans, letting Chinese women and families enter the country would threaten a "white man's country."

Before the Chinese Exclusion Act, however, some men had been able to bring their wives to America, or to have women sent over to become their wives. One such man was Chin Gee Hee, who arrived in Washington Territory in 1862 and found work in a lumber mill. Within a few years he sent for his wife and got her a job in the mill's cookhouse. Their son, Chin Lem, was born in 1875. He is believed to be the first Chinese American born in Washington.

Another Chinese wife braved the difficulties of traveling across the Pacific to join her husband in California, where she sewed garments and made cigarettes to support herself and her child while her husband worked in the mines.

Slowly, Chinese families began to form as men left the mines and railroad crews for more stable jobs in farming or shopkeeping. In the early decades, however, most of the Chinese women who came to America came alone, often brought by force to serve as prostitutes. Some sank into opium addiction or died from abuse or disease. Many of them, however, managed to buy their way out of servitude. Marriage and children became possibilities for them because there were so few Chinese women available.

(left) Chinese Americans in a tenement in San Francisco's Chinatown, around 1890.

A Colony of Bachelors

A big problem for Chinese men was that there were not enough Chinese women. The Exclusion Act outlawed the immigration of Chinese women as well as laborers. After the Act was passed, the prospect of bringing a wife to America disappeared for most Chinese men. For the overwhelming majority of these immigrants, the future would not include a family in their adopted land. They became a colony of bachelors, men who had never married or who had left their wives in China and now could not bring them to America.

The Chinese had come to America with the idea of making a temporary stay, but from the beginning they showed signs of settling down. Chinatown in San Francisco was already a bustling colony in the 1850s, with dozens of stores selling Chinese groceries, clothing, medicines, and other goods for the ethnic community. New arrivals from China were drawn to the neighborhood. By the mid-1870s Chinatown was six blocks long, busy and vibrant. Immigrants also built Chinatowns in rural towns like Sacramento, Marysville, and Stockton, with businesses to serve the needs of Chinese miners and farmers.

Organizations were part of life in Chinese

America from the start. Groups called *tongs* not only controlled criminal enterprises such as prostitution and gambling but also protected Chinese migrants. Other organizations called *fongs* were made up of family or village members. Clans were larger groups of fongs. These associations maintained clubhouses that served as residences and social centers for members. They established temples, helped people send letters home to China, and shipped the bodies of the dead back to the homeland for burial. The fongs and clans also helped new arrivals find housing and jobs.

Gradually, the Chinese were creating their own communities in America. They celebrated their own holidays and enjoyed performances at Chinese theaters. The many unmarried men gathered in social clubs and in the back rooms of stores, passing their lonely hours together in conversation and gambling, sharing letters from the villages and families in China that they would never see again.

An Earthquake Brings a Change in Fortune

Desperate to bring their wives and children to America, Chinese men looked for loopholes in the law. Laborers' families could not immigrate, but the families of merchants could enter the country, so many laundrymen, restaurant owners, and other workers tried to pass themselves off as merchants. Still, most Chinese men thought that they would never be able to bring their wives to America. Then suddenly a natural disaster changed the course of Chinese American history.

Early in the morning of April 18, 1906, an earthquake shook San Francisco. Residents of Chinatown fled in terror from collapsing buildings. Then fires swept through the devastated city. Among the many things that were destroyed in the disaster were most of the city's records. That opened the way for a new Chinese immigration.

Although Chinese immigrants could not become citizens, anyone born in the United States was automatically a citizen, no matter what his or her race. After the disaster, Chinese men who had immigrated could claim that they had been born in San Francisco—and they could not be expected to prove it, because everyone knew that birth certificates and citizenship records had been destroyed by the fire. And once a man was recognized as a US citizen, he could bring his wife and children from China.

After the catastrophe in San Francisco, Chinese women began arriving in increasing numbers. Between 1910 and 1924, one in four Chinese immigrants was female, compared with only one in twenty before 1900. By 1930 women accounted for one-fifth of the total Chinese population in America, providing the basis for Chinese American families.

Chinese sons also began coming to America at this time. According to US law, children of American citizens were also American citizens, even if they were born in a different country. This meant that children in China who had been fathered by Chinese American citizens could enter the United States.

Many of the young men who immigrated really were the sons of US citizens. But others were the sons of men who only pretended to be citizens, claiming that their birth certificates had been destroyed. Still others were not sons at all—they paid Chinese Americans to claim them as sons. The young men who entered the country under false pretenses were called "paper sons" because their citizenship existed only on paper.

By the thousands, Chinese began entering the United States again. After passing through the narrow waterway called the Golden Gate, they left

their ships at an immigration station on Angel
Island in San Francisco Bay. There they were
crowded into unsanitary barracks to await their
entrance interviews. By 1943, some fifty thousand
Chinese had entered America through Angel
Island.

"Caught in Between": Born in America

From Angel Island the newcomers went to the
cities, seeking shelter, and employment in the
Chinatowns of Los Angeles, Oakland, Chicago,
Seattle, Portland, New York, and Boston as well
as San Francisco. Although there were Chinese
in nearly all parts of the United States, the cities
of San Francisco and New York were home to 40
percent of all Chinese in America by 1940.

Chinatowns became residential communities, business districts, and tourist centers. They
also became places where children lived. In 1900
children were relatively rare in the nation's Chinatowns. Only 11 percent of the Chinese population
had been born in America. "The greatest impression I have of my childhood in those days was
that at that time there were very few families in
Chinatown," one resident recalled. "Babies were

looked on with a kind of wonder." But thanks in part to the San Francisco earthquake and fire, the American-born Chinese group grew quickly to 41 percent of the population in 1930 and 52 percent in 1940.

In their Chinatown world, children watched their parents work long hours. Young children accompanied their parents to the factory—one Chinese American man remembered being tied to his mother's back while she operated a sewing machine in a garment shop. The children were urged by their parents to study hard so they could have better lives.

For the second-generation Chinese Americans, education was viewed as a way to advance in society. Yet at home, two cultures sometimes clashed. Young people simply wanted more independence and more choice for themselves than their traditional parents allowed. Many youngsters experienced painfully torn feelings, pulled by their ethnic identity and by their desire to fit into the larger American society.

"There was endless discussion about what to do about the dilemma of being caught in between . . . being loyal to the parents and their ways and yet trying to assess the good from both sides," said

Victor Wong, a second-generation Chinese American. "We used to call ourselves just a 'marginal man,' caught between two cultures."

TESTING THE
"PAPER SONS"

MANY YOUNG CHINESE MEN TRIED TO ENTER THE
United States as "paper sons." They pretended to
be the sons of Chinese men who were American
citizens because they had been born in the United
States. The claim alone was not enough to get the
paper sons into the country. They were tested to
see if they really were the children of the men they
called their "fathers."

During the sea voyage from China, the hopeful
paper sons studied lists of the things they were
supposed to know, such as the names and birth-
days of everyone in their so-called families. When
the ship approached the Golden Gate and the
entrance to San Francisco Bay, the men tore up
their lists and threw them overboard.

Jim Quock paid for a "citizen paper" and
was given a 200-page book to memorize, full of
details about his "family." When Quock arrived
at the immigration station on Angel Island in
San Francisco, he was held for three weeks to be
interviewed. He was asked all kinds of questions,

including "How many steps are there in your house?" and "Where do you sleep?"

Sometimes paper sons had to think quickly. Two young men who were supposed to be brothers applied to enter the United States as sons of a Chinese American merchant. The examiners interviewed them separately and asked each of them if there were a dog in their house. One applicant said yes, the other no. Confronted with these results, the first applicant said smartly, "Yes, well, we had a dog, but we knew we were coming to the United States, so we ate the dog."

Paper sons were not released until they had convinced the examiners that their papers were authentic. Those who failed the test were forced to return to China. The lucky ones were allowed to hurry onto ferries and sail happily to San Francisco.

CHAPTER NINE

DEALING WITH THE INDIANS

ONE OF THE MOST SIGNIFICANT events of the 1890s in the United States was the end of the frontier. In 1891 the US Census Bureau announced that Americans had settled the entire continent, and that the frontier had come to an end. Two years later a historian named Frederick Jackson Turner published a thesis that would make him famous.

Turner's thesis was titled "The Significance of the Frontier in American History." It said that America and its people had been shaped by the great historic movement of advancing the frontier, which Turner called "the meeting point between savagery and civilization." Conquering the frontier had made Americans strong and self-reliant, producing a new civilization that was different from any other.

These ideas supported the popular but inaccurate story that says that the United States was settled by Europeans, and that Americans are white. With this view of history, it was inevitable that the Native Americans would be overcome and replaced by white Americans. The conquest of those first inhabitants was a necessary part of the taming and civilizing of the land.

The official closing of the frontier in 1891, many people thought at the time, marked the triumph of civilization. An event the year before, however, had showed the tragic cost of that triumph.

The Massacre at Wounded Knee

In 1889 an Indian prophet emerged from the shores of Pyramid Lake in Nevada. He was Wovoka of the Paiute tribe, and he called on Native Americans everywhere to perform a ceremony he called the Ghost Dance, wearing "ghost shirts" decorated with sacred symbols of blue and yellow lines. Wovoka claimed that the Ghost Dance would bring about the return of Indian ways, the restoration of the buffalo, and Indian control of their former lands.

"All Indians must dance, everywhere, keep on dancing. . . . The game [will] be thick everywhere.

All dead Indians [will] come back and live again,"
Wovoka said. His vision of a world without whites
spread like a prairie fire through Indian country.
Ghost dancing seized hold of the Sioux reservations. In the winter of 1890 a government agent at
Pine Ridge Reservation in South Dakota told his
superiors in Washington, "Indians are dancing in
the snow and are wild and crazy. We need protection and we need it now."

The Indian Bureau in Washington ordered the
army to arrest several Sioux leaders, including
Chiefs Sitting Bull and Big Foot. When Indian
policemen arrested Sitting Bull, a scuffle broke out
with his followers, and the police shot and killed
the chief. Alarmed by this news, Big Foot tried to
escape with his people. When the cavalry caught
them, the Indians surrendered. The soldiers
took them to a camp near a frozen creek called
Wounded Knee.

The following morning the Indians were ordered
to turn over their weapons. Then soldiers began
searching the tepees, and the situation grew tense.
When a medicine man began dancing the Ghost
Dance, a shot rang out, and suddenly the soldiers
were firing on the unarmed Indians. "There were
only about a hundred warriors and there were

nearly five hundred soldiers," a survivor named Black Elk recalled. "The warriors rushed to where they had piled their guns and knives."

Artillery guns fired from a ridge overlooking the camp took a terrible toll on the Indians. Those who fled from the camp were chased down by soldiers. "Dead and wounded women and children and little babies were scattered all along there where they had been trying to run away," Black Elk reported. "The soldiers had followed them along the gulch, as they ran, and murdered them in there."

When the guns stopped spewing their deadly fire, a terrible silence descended on the bloody scene. Hundreds of Indians lay dead or wounded on the icy ground, along with many soldiers, most of whom had been shot in the chaos by weapons fired by their own side. Heavy snow began to fall. After the storm passed, the soldiers threw the Indian bodies into a long trench for mass burial, stripping the ghost shirts from the dancers' bodies as souvenirs.

Custer and the Frontier

Before Wounded Knee there was the massacre at the Washita River in Oklahoma, in the winter of 1868. Lieutenant Colonel George Armstrong Custer and eight hundred soldiers had been tracking a band of Cheyenne Indians when they came upon an Indian camp in the darkness. Custer ordered his men to surround it. At dawn they attacked, destroying the lodges, killing more than a hundred men, and capturing more than fifty women and children. Custer and his men marched triumphantly back to their own camp waving the scalps of the Cheyenne men and their leader, Chief Black Kettle.

Eight years later, Custer—who had been promoted to general—met his own violent death at the Battle of the Little Big Horn River in the Montana Territory. Surrounded by the Lakota and Cheyenne warriors of Chief Crazy Horse, Custer refused to surrender. He and all his men were killed.

Custer was famous as an Indian fighter, yet he identified with the Indians in many ways. He loved the freedom of the frontier and the beauty of the Western wilderness, and he wrote that if he were an Indian, he would choose the "free open plains" rather than the "confined limits of a reservation."

The Reservation System

Unlike Custer, Francis A. Walker tried to avoid using armed force against the Indians. Walker was the federal government's Commissioner of Indian Affairs in the 1870s. He recommended that soldiers should not surprise Indian camps at night and should not shoot down men, women, and children. Instead, he wanted the government to pursue peace by buying off the Indians to avoid violent conflict.

Walker had little experience with Indians, but he had confidence in the civilizing forces of technology and commerce. He saw that progress was bringing an end to the frontier, as railways crossed the continent and Americans migrated in ever-larger numbers into the Great Plains. Indians faced a grim future in this rapidly changing world. Walker felt that his mission was to save the Indians, making sure that they survived until they were ready to enter civilization. He believed in social engineering—in other words, he thought that the government should scientifically manage the welfare of Indians, for their own good.

Industrial progress had cut off the Indians from their traditional ways of making a livelihood. So, Walker argued, the government should support them temporarily until they mastered new ways. His plan for this transition was to move the Indians of the West into one or two large reservations, leaving the land outside these reservations open for white settlement. Indians outside the reservation boundaries would be fair game to be attacked by the military at any time.

The long-term goal, Walker explained, was to help the Native American people assimilate. He pictured the giant reservation as a place where Indians would have to work, learn industrial skills, attend school, and generally do as they were told. A program of education and work would turn the former wanderers into settled laborers. Trained and reformed on the reservation, the Indians would be prepared to enter civilized society.

The Dawes Act

Other white reformers had a different solution to the question of what to do with the Indians. In their view, reservations only kept Native Americans apart from the rest of society and delayed their assimilation. This view became official policy in 1887, when Congress passed the Dawes Act.

The Dawes Act reversed Walker's Peace Policy.

It was designed to break up the reservations that already existed and to turn Indians into individual property owners and US citizens. Reservation lands belonged to tribes, not to individuals, but the Dawes Act gave the president the power, without tribal consent, to give land to individual families in plots of up to 160 acres. These parcels were called allotments. Any "surplus" reservation land that was left after individuals had received their allotments could be sold by the government to white settlers. Profits from these sales would go toward educating the Indians, who would become US citizens when they accepted their allotments.

Senator Henry Dawes, the author of the act, believed that for the Indians to be civilized the tribal system must be destroyed. Owning communal land led to savage habits and laziness. By creating private property holders, the allotment system would make Indians independent and self-reliant. Selling the "surplus" reservation land to whites would help the Indians, too. Native American farmers would learn good work habits from the white farmers who would be their neighbors.

The Dawes Act gave Indians what they already owned: their land. But it also took land away from them. White farmers and business interests were well aware of the economic advantages they stood to gain from the allotment program. In 1880, Secretary of the Interior Carl Schurz predicted that the allotments would "eventually open to settlement by white men the large tracts of land now belonging to the reservations, but not used by the Indians."

Railroad companies also benefited from the policy of breaking up reservations. In 1886–1887, Congress made six land grants to railroad interests, giving them the right to build railways through Indian land and to claim property along the railway lines. During the next two sessions of Congress, the nation's lawmakers granted another twenty-three railroad rights-of-way through Indian territories.

Land Changes Hands

Four years after the Dawes Act became law, Indian Commissioner Thomas Morgan calculated that in the year 1891 alone, one-seventh of all Indian lands were sold to non-Indians. While Morgan admitted that this might look like a rapid loss of land, he explained that the Indians had hardly used it and did not need it.

In 1902 Congress passed a new law that sped up the transfer of land from Indians to whites. The law said that when the Indian owner of a land allotment died, the property could not be left to the owner's heirs but had to be sold at open auction. Unless the heirs were able to buy their own family land, they would lose it. A government official assured President Theodore Roosevelt that under this system "it will be but a few years at most before all the Indians' land will have passed into the possession of the settlers."

Native Americans resisted these efforts to take their lands away. Chief Lone Wolf of the Kiowa, for example, insisted in court that an 1868 treaty required that all deals involving tribal land must be approved by the whole tribe. The US Supreme Court ruled against him, saying that the federal government had the power to change or cancel the provisions of an Indian treaty. This decision allowed the government to dispose of Indians' land without their permission. One Indian Affairs official greeted the decision with relief, saying that without the Supreme Court it might have taken as long as fifty years to get rid of the reservations and free up the land for white farmers.

By 1933 the Native American peoples of the

United States had lost about 60 percent of the 138 million acres they had owned at the time of the Dawes Act. The policy of allotment had been turning the Indians into a landless people.

A Change in Direction

The allotment program was halted suddenly in 1934 by a new law called the Indian Reorganization Act. This Act was the creation of John Collier, who had been named Commissioner of Indian Affairs by President Franklin D. Roosevelt.

Collier admired the sense of community he found among the Native American peoples of New Mexico. He declared that only the Indians still knew the secret of building character through communal life. Collier wanted to let Indians remain Indians and allow them to enter modern life without giving up their heritage and culture. "If the Indian life is a good life," he wrote, "then we should be proud and glad to have this different and native culture going on by the side of ours."

In Collier's view, allotment was destroying the Indian communal way of life. His Indian Reorganization Act represented a complete change in direction from the Dawes Act. It not only ended the allotment program but also authorized the use of federal funds for tribes to buy land and establish their own local self-governments. This reorganization, though, would apply only to tribes in which a majority of members voted to accept it. No tribe would be forced to reorganize. Collier felt that letting the tribes choose whether or not to change from one system to the other was a way of giving Indians some say in their destiny.

A year after the new law went into effect, 172 tribes with a total of 132,426 members voted to accept reorganization. Another 73 tribes with a total of 63,467 voted not to be included in the reorganization.

The Navajos' Long Walk

The Navajo of the Southwest were one of the tribes that turned down the offer of reorganization. To them, Collier represented a long tradition of white people telling Indians what was in their best interest.

The Navajo remembered decisions that whites had made for them in the 1860s. For several centuries, ever since they acquired sheep from the Spanish, the Navajo had been herders. After the United States won the Southwest in the war against Mexico, whites began intruding on Navajo lands. Conflict followed.

In 1863 the Navajo surrendered to an army scout named Christopher "Kit" Carson after his troops destroyed their orchards and sheep herds. The Indians were rounded up and marched to a reservation called Bosque Redondo. They called this event the Long Walk. Five years later, the government moved the Navajo again—to a reservation in their original homeland. The Indians also received sheep to replace the livestock Carson's forces had destroyed.

Now, in the 1930s, the Navajo were getting instructions not from a soldier like Carson but from a government administrator. Although Collier wanted to give the Indians self-rule, he was also trying to socially engineer their world—he even called it an ethnic laboratory. The Navajos rejected his reorganization plan because they did not want an outside "guardian" telling them what was best for them.

The reorganization vote was only one of Collier's interactions with the Navajo. In 1933 he decided that the Navajo owned half a million more livestock than their reservation could support. Overgrazing by their sheep and goats, he claimed, was causing severe soil erosion. Unless

the problem of erosion was solved, and soon, the sheep-raising Navajo would experience great hardship and suffering.

Collier was worried about Navajo survival, but he was also worried about white interests. He had received reports that silt from erosion on Navajo land was filling the Colorado River and threatening to clog Boulder Dam (now called Hoover Dam), a huge hydroelectric project that was being built to supply water to California's agricultural heartland and to provide electricity for Los Angeles. The United States Geological Survey identified the Navajo reservation as the chief cause of the Colorado silt problem.

The solution, Collier decided, was to reduce Navajo livestock by 400,000 animals. Over a five-year period he flew to the reservation seventeen times to explain and promote the stock reduction program, but the Navajo did not accept it. "In my long life of social effort and struggle," Collier later wrote, "I have not experienced among any other Indian group, or any group whatsoever, an anxiety-ridden and anguished hostility even approaching that which the Navajo were undergoing."

(left) The federal government and the Navajo clashed over the issue of sheep, which had long been central to Navajo life.

Erosion

For the Navajo, sheep and survival were the same. Raising sheep was their way of life. Boys grew up caring for the flocks, and herding represented the closeness of the family and the passing of values from one generation to the next. Reducing their herds went against everything they believed, everything they had learned from years of living on their land.

But Collier carried out his program to remove livestock in order to stop erosion. Agents removed sheep and goats while the Navajo wondered how they would live without their stock. After his sheep had been taken away, one herder cursed the officials: "You people are indeed heartless. You have now killed me. You have cut off my arms. You have cut off my legs. You have taken my head off. There is nothing left for me. This is the end of the trail."

Meanwhile, the Navajo found themselves increasingly living on wages, mostly from temporary government employment. The stock reduction program had reduced many Navajo to dependency on the federal government. To the Indians, Collier's project was the most devastating experience in their tribal history since the Long Walk.

Tragically, the stock reduction program was not even necessary to control erosion. After more research on soil erosion, scientists would discover that overgrazing was not the source of the problem. The Navajo had known that all along, and had tried in vain to tell the government. They knew that erosion had occurred many times in the past. It was part of a years-long cycle of dry weather, erosion, rainfall, and recovery. The problems of erosion and silt had more to do with drought than with the number of Navajo livestock.

The 1930s had brought years of little rain. The Indians predicted that the dry rangelands would be covered with fresh new grass when the drought ended. But by that time, sadly, their herds and their way of life would be eroded along with the soil.

THE LAST ARROW

"LAST-ARROW PAGEANTS" WERE EVENTS THAT
the federal government organized to symbolize
the Native Americans' shift from their old way
of life to a new life as landowners and farmers.
An article from the *Gettysburg Times* of January 5,
1917, describes how the Department of the Interior
held these ceremonies "to modernize the race" of
Indians:

> *The Indians who are to be honored with the*
> *confidence of the government are selected by*
> *a "competency commission" of three men . . .*
> *who go through a reservation from house*
> *to house, reporting on the progress of each*
> *family—the condition of the house and farm,*
> *the way the children are cared for and their*
> *general economic status. . . . [T]he Indians*
> *selected are invited to a public meeting. . . .*
>
> *There a representative of the department*
> *of the interior tells them very solemnly that*
> *the president has heard that they are ready*
> *to leave the control of the Indian bureau and*
> *become free American citizens. . . . He then*
> *calls the English name of the first man on his*

*list—James Robinson, it may be, whose Indian
name, perhaps, was Rain-in-the-Face. . . .*

*[T]he official hands him a bow and arrow,
telling him to shoot the arrow. The Indian
complies.*

*As the arrow strikes the ground the
representative of the government says: "Rain-
in-the-Face, you have shot your last arrow.
That means that you are no longer to live the
life of an Indian. You are from this day forward
to live the life of a white man. But you may
keep that arrow. It will be to you a symbol of
your noble race and of the pride you feel that
you come from the first of all Americans.*

*"James Robinson, take in your hand this
plow."*

The government official then told the Indian that
the plow represented work. Another gift, a purse,
represented savings, and the official urged the
Indian to work hard and use his earnings wisely.
The third gift, a flag, represented American citizenship.

"The general effect of the ceremonial has proved
most happy," says the final sentence of the article,
"and the honor of participating in it has served as

a stimulus to many of the Indians to work harder for the privileges of citizenship." Nowhere does the article say what the Indians themselves thought about this ceremony, or of the way it required them to give up the names and customs of their people.

CHAPTER TEN

THE JAPANESE AND "MONEY TREES"

WHILE THE FRONTIER WAS BEING declared closed in 1890, America was receiving a new group of immigrants: the Japanese. Like the Irish and the Chinese, the Japanese were pushed toward the United States by forces that made life difficult in their homeland.

In the middle of the nineteenth century, America's influence reached across the Pacific. US naval ships had entered Tokyo Bay in 1853 and forcefully opened Japan's doors to the rest of the world. Meanwhile, Western powers were busy colonizing China. To prevent the same thing from happening in their country, Japan's leaders established a strong central government in 1868. The Japanese government launched programs to develop the country's industrial and military might. Heavy taxes on the people paid for these programs.

Bearing the burden of taxation, Japanese farmers suffered severe economic hardship during the 1880s. Thousands of farmers were forced to sell their land to pay their taxes and debts. Hunger stalked many parts of the country. Searching for a way out of their plight, impoverished farmers were seized with emigration fever.

Fabulous stories of high wages abroad stirred their imaginations. A plantation laborer in Hawaii could earn six times more than in Japan. In three years, a worker in Hawaii might manage to save as much as he could earn in ten years in Japan. Stories about wages in the mainland United States seemed even more fantastic. No wonder young men begged their parents to let them go to America. They exclaimed, "In America, money grew on trees."

Between 1885 and 1924, hundreds of thousands of Japanese left their homeland. About 200,000 Japanese went to Hawaii, and another 180,000 went to the US mainland. One migrant captured their excitement in the traditional Japanese form of poetry called haiku:

> *Huge dreams of fortune*
> *Go with me to foreign lands,*
> *Across the ocean.*

Picture Brides

Like the Chinese, the Japanese crossed the Pacific driven by dreams of making money. But there was a significant difference between the two migrations. Most of the Chinese immigrants were men, but the Japanese flow to America included an abundance of women.

By 1920, women made up 46 percent of the Japanese in Hawaii and 35 percent in California, compared with only 5 percent for the Chinese. Why the difference?

Unlike China, Japan was ruled by a strong central government that could regulate emigration. Hearing that the mostly male Chinese community in America had problems with prostitution, gambling, and drunkenness, the Japanese government hoped to prevent the same problems among its own emigrants by promoting the emigration of women. Men with wives and families, government leaders reasoned, would be more likely to lead settled, productive lives and not give the Japanese people a bad name. The Hawaiian government shared these views and encouraged married couples and women to immigrate.

In addition, Japanese women were less bound by tradition than Chinese women. Japan's move toward an industrial economy had brought women into the workforce as construction workers, coal miners, and laborers in textile factories. By 1900, three-fifths of Japan's industrial laborers were women. And because Japan's new government required girls as well as boys to attend school, Japanese women were more likely than Chinese women to be educated and to know how to read and write. Starting in 1876, many learned English in school. These factors may have paved the way for women to consider working in America.

A loophole in American immigration policy also favored Japanese women. Under a 1907 arrangement called the Gentlemen's Agreement, the United States allowed Japanese immigrants to bring their family members to join them. Some sixty thousand women came to America this way. Many of them were "picture brides," women who had been joined through arranged marriages to men they had never met.

Arranged marriages were an established custom in Japan. Marriage was considered not an individual choice but a family concern, and parents consulted go-betweens to help them select partners for their sons and daughters. After the invention of photography, the exchange of pictures became part of this practice. When a potential bride and groom did not live near each other, they would exchange photographs before they met.

This custom was well suited to the needs of Japanese migrants. Men who had gone to America could exchange pictures through the mail with women in Japan. Their families would arrange long-distance marriages, after which the new brides would be able to enter the United States to join their husbands.

As they prepared to leave for Hawaii or the US mainland, many women felt anxious about separating from their homes in Japan. One woman remembered that when her husband's brother said farewell, he added, "Don't stay in the States too long. Come back in five years and farm with us."

"Are you kidding?" her father quickly said. "They can't learn anything in five years. They'll even have a baby over there. . . . Be patient for twenty years." Her father's words shocked her. Suddenly she realized how long the separation could be.

Working in Hawaii

Hawaii was a kingdom until 1900, when it became a territory of the United States. Even before 1900, American planters had developed a successful sugarcane industry in the Hawaiian Islands, producing sugar for export. Between 1875 and 1910, land under cultivation in the islands increased from 12,000 to 214,000 acres. To work this land, the planters needed laborers. Their chief source was Japan, but it was not their only source.

The planters paid attention to the nationalities of their workers. They systemically developed a labor force that was ethnically diverse, so that they could create divisions among the workers. This kept the workers from uniting and made it easier for management to control them. A plantation manager told how to avoid workers' strikes: "Keep a variety of laborers, that is different nationalities, and thus prevent any concerted action in case of strikes, for there are few, if any, cases of Japs, Chinese, and Portuguese entering into a strike as a unit." Planters also imported laborers from Korea and the Philippines in order to pit them against the Japanese, hoping that this would keep Japanese workers from making demands.

To strengthen their authority over this ethnically

diverse workforce, planters created a status system of tasks based on race. Whites occupied the supervisory and skilled positions. Asians did unskilled fieldwork. In 1904, the Hawaiian Sugar Planters' Association passed a resolution saying that only US citizens, or people eligible to become citizens, could hold skilled positions. This ruled out Asians, because only white people were allowed to become naturalized US citizens at that time.

"I haven't got a chance," one Japanese worker told an interviewer, explaining his frustration with racial discrimination. "You can't go very high up and get big money unless your skin is white. You can work here all your life and yet a haole [white person] who doesn't know a thing about the work can be ahead of you in no time."

Tears in the Cane Fields

On the plantations, Japanese workers found themselves in a regimented world, not an organized world. Early in the morning they were jarred out of sleep by the loud scream of the plantation siren. Foremen strode through the camps, knocking on doors and shouting at the workers to get up. In gangs of twenty to thirty, the workers were marched to the fields. Some gangs were made up of just one nationality. Others included Japanese, Puerto Rican, Filipino, Chinese, Portuguese, and Hawaiian laborers.

There were gangs of women workers, too. In 1920, 14 percent of the plantation labor force was female, mostly Japanese. Women were concentrated in certain kinds of fieldwork: hoeing, stripping leaves from the canes, and harvesting. Although they were given many of the same assignments as male workers, women were paid less. Female field hands received an average wage of fifty-five cents a day in 1915, compared with seventy-eight cents for male hands.

Around the neck of each worker was a chain with a small brass disk. On each disk was a number, or *bango*. Field bosses, or *lunas*, called the workers by this number. In the old country, names had connected these men and women to family and community, but in the cane fields they became numbers.

A luna, often on horseback, surveyed the whole scene. "If we talked too much the man swung his whip," one Japanese laborer recalled. "He did not actually whip us but just swung his whip so that we would work harder."

Fieldwork was punishingly difficult. Hoeing weeds was both boring and backbreaking. Workers moved for hours in a straight line without talking. Harvesting the cane with mechanical swings of a machete was dirty and exhausting. It resulted in blistered hands and arms scratched by the saw-blade edges of the cane leaves. Twelve feet tall, the cane enclosed the workers, who sweated from the terrible heat and humidity. Surrounded by red dust, they cov-

(above) Japanese sugarcane worker, Maui, Hawaii, 1932.

ered their faces with handkerchiefs. A song summed up a woman worker's experience in the field:

> *My husband cuts the cane stalks*
> *And I trim their leaves*
> *With sweat and tears we both work*
> *For our means.*

After collecting the cane stalks, the workers tied them into bundles and loaded them onto railway cars. A train carried the stalks to the mill, where they were crushed and their juices were boiled. Inside the mill, laborers worked amid heat, steam, and the constant loud clanking and whirring of machinery.

Workers United

Contrary to the stereotype of Japanese immigrants as quiet and ready to accept anything, Japanese laborers in Hawaii aggressively protested against unfair labor conditions. They often engaged in strikes. At first, laborers of different groups tended to think in terms of ethnicity, rather than seeing that workers of all ethnic groups shared the same struggle. Japanese workers, for example, organized themselves into "blood unions" based on their ethnic identity.

The most important action of the blood unions was the Japanese strike of 1909. Pointing out that Portuguese workers received $22.50 a month while Japanese workers got only $18 a month for the same work, the Japanese called for higher wages and an end to racial inequality in pay. Several thousand Japanese plantation laborers halted work on the island of Oahu. Fellow Japanese on the other islands sent support in the form of money and food. Japanese businesses also aided the strikers, and the Japanese Physicians Association gave free medical care to the strikers and their families.

The strike showed that the workers were beginning to think of themselves as permanent settlers, not temporary visitors. They were becoming Japanese Americans. In their demand for a higher wage they explained that they wanted to "unite our destiny with that of Hawaii, sharing the prosperity and adversity of Hawaii with other citizens of Hawaii."

The planters responded by pressuring the government to arrest the strike leaders for conspiracy. Then they hired Chinese, Hawaiian, Portuguese, and Filipino workers as "scabs"—laborers who would break the strike by doing the strikers' jobs. The strikers held out for four months before they were forced to return to work.

The Japanese strikers had won a victory, for soon afterward the planters raised their wages and ended the system of different wages for different races. Yet after the strike was broken, the planters began importing massive numbers of Filipino workers. By 1920 the labor force was 30 percent Filipino and only 44 percent Japanese.

Workers of both nationalities began to realize that the labor movement in Hawaii would have to be based on working-class unity across ethnic lines. When the Filipino union went on strike in 1920, the Japanese union joined the strike. This work stoppage by eight thousand people—77 percent of the plantation workforce on Oahu—brought sugar production to a standstill. The Japanese union questioned the wisdom of having separate, ethnic labor organizations. It proposed one union for "laborers of all nationalities."

Divide and Control

Confronted by the prospect of workers uniting,

the planters turned to their time-tested strategy of divide and control. They promoted distrust between the Filipino and Japanese communities and offered a bribe to Filipino union leader Pablo Manlapit. Both Filipino and Japanese workers were surprised when Manlapit suddenly called off the strike, calling it a Japanese action to cripple Hawaii's economy—even though the Filipino union had been the first to strike.

Many Filipino union members defied Manlapit and continued to strike. The planters stepped up their attack with propaganda claiming that the Japanese strikers were puppets of the Japanese government, which planned to "Japanise" Hawaii. The planters hired Hawaiians, Portuguese, and Koreans as strikebreakers, and they evicted the striking workers from their homes on the plantations.

Forced to take shelter in Honolulu's vacant lots, homeless during the height of a flu epidemic, thousands of workers and their family members became ill. One hundred and fifty died. Tired, hungry, and sick, the strikers gave up their struggle in July. The planters claimed a victory—but three months later they quietly raised wages by 50 percent.

Ethnic Communities

On the plantations, workers of different nationalities were usually housed in separate camps. The early camps were generally crowded and unsanitary, with as many as fifty workers living under one roof. But over time, as planters replaced single workers with married men, the barracks were replaced by cottages for families. The planters had learned that it was in their own best interests to make the workers more comfortable. "Pleasant surroundings, with some of the modern comforts and conveniences," said one plantation official, "go a long way to make the worker healthier and more efficient in his work."

Meanwhile, the workers were turning their camps into ethnic communities. On every plantation, Japanese immigrants established Buddhist temples and Japanese-language schools for their children. They held traditional celebrations such as the midsummer *obon*, or festival of souls, when they dressed in kimonos and danced in circles to the beat of taiko drums to honor the reunion of the living with the spirits of the dead.

At first, the laborers of each ethnic group spoke only their native language. This gave each group a sense of community within its camp, letting members maintain ties with each other and with their culture as they shared memories and experiences. Soon, though, workers of different groups began to acquire a common language. Planters wanted workers to know basic English, the language in which commands were given. A plantation dialect called "Pidgin English" developed—simple English that also included Hawaiian, Japanese, Portuguese, and Chinese phrases and rhythms.

Pidgin had begun as a language of command, but it soon became the language of community. "The language we used had to be either Pidgin English or broken English," said a Filipino worker, explaining how different groups communicated with each other on the plantation. "And when we don't understand each other, we had to add some other words that would help to explain ourselves. That's how this Pidgin English comes out beautiful."

As Pidgin English became the language of the camps, it let people from different countries communicate with each other, helping them create a new identity that was tied to Hawaii. The use of a new language reflected a deeper change in how they saw themselves and their place. They had come to Hawaii planning to earn money and then return to Japan, and many did return. Of the 200,000 Japanese who entered Hawaii between 1885 and 1924, about 110,000, or 55 percent of them, went home. What is significant, though, is that almost half stayed.

A New Generation

Gradually, over the years, Japanese workers found themselves establishing families in their new Hawaiian home. In 1920 nearly half the Japanese in Hawaii were just nineteen years old or younger. The immigrants were planting roots through their children.

Some immigrants with children considered returning to Japan but found themselves unable to do so. In a letter to his brother, Asakichi Inouye explained that he had decided not to return to Japan because his children were settled in Hawaii, and so was his grandson Daniel (who would later be elected to the US Senate). Inouye feared that he and his wife would not find contentment in their old home in Japan.

Something similar happened to Shokichi and Matsu Fukuda. They had emigrated from Japan together in 1900 to work on the Hawaiian island of Maui. Twenty years later they decided to go back to Japan and take their Hawaiian-born children with them. Their teenage son, however, refused to go. Hawaii was his home, the only world he knew, and he wanted the family to stay there.

Seeing their parents suffering from backbreaking work, low wages, and discrimination, many second-generation Japanese Americans refused to be forced into plantation labor. Education, they believed, was the key to job opportunities and freedom from the plantation. They wanted to be something more than field laborers.

The planters did not want the immigrants' children to receive too much education. They needed the second generation as plantation laborers. Sixth or maybe eighth grade, they felt, was enough. Young people stayed in school, however, and learned about the American ideals of democracy and equality. Returning from school to their camps, they saw whites on the top and Asians on the bottom, and they began to question the plantation system.

Japanese immigrants had labored to build the great sugar industry in Hawaii. Their sweat and tears had watered the cane fields. As they learned Pidgin English and watched their children grow up in the camps and attend American schools, they realized that they had become settlers, and that Hawaii had become their home.

With one woven basket
Alone I came
Now I have children
And even grandchildren too.

Transforming California

During a visit to California in the 1920s, a young Japanese man from Hawaii was shocked by the strong anti-Japanese hostility he encountered. Although he had heard rumors about how badly whites treated Japanese on the US mainland, reality was a shock:

> *But I didn't realize the true situation until I had a personal experience. In one instance, I went to a barbershop to get my hair trimmed. On entering the shop, one of the barbers approached me and asked for my nationality. I answered that I was Japanese, and as soon as he heard that I was of the yellow race, he drove me out of the place as if he were driving away a cat or a dog.*

In Hawaii, 40 percent of the population was

Japanese in 1920. On the mainland, however, the Japanese were a tiny racial minority. They totaled just 2 percent of the population in California. Scorned by white society, they had become the targets of hostile and violent white workers.

Most of the immigrants had been farmers in Japan. For centuries their families had cultivated small plots, irrigating the land and relying on intensive labor to make it productive. To become farmers in America was their dream. Although Japanese immigrants also worked at first as field hands, on railroad construction, and in canneries, many became farmers. They raised crops for white landowners, rented land, and, once they had saved enough money, bought land of their own.

The Japanese immigrants entered American agriculture at a time of change. Beginning in the late nineteenth century, the rise of industry and the growth of cities had created a demand for fresh produce in the nation's urban centers. At the same time, irrigation expanded greatly in California, opening the way for intensive agriculture—orchards and gardens as opposed to vast wheat fields or pastures that required little water. Two important technological developments—railway lines and the refrigerated railway car—made it possible for California's farmers to ship perishable fruits and vegetables to almost anywhere in the United States.

Japanese farmers came onto this scene at the right time, and they rapidly flourished. In 1900 California's Japanese farmers owned or rented twenty-nine farms, totaling 4,698 acres. Within five years the acreage farmed by the Japanese had jumped to 61,858. By 1920 Japanese farmers were cultivating nearly half a million acres, growing large percentages of the strawberries, onions, tomatoes, celery, snap beans, and green peas that were produced in the state. That year the production of Japanese farms was valued at $67 million, about 10 percent of the total value of California's crops.

Workdays on the farms were long and demanding—especially for women, who had the double duty of fieldwork and housework. Still, driven by their dreams of rich harvests, these pioneering Japanese men and women turned the dusty Sacramento Valley and the deserts of the Imperial Valley into lush and profitable fields and orchards.

One of the most successful Japanese farmers was Kinji Ushijima, better known as George Shima, who came to California in 1887. He worked as a potato picker, then a labor contractor,

and then a farmer. Shima leased and bought unde-
veloped swamplands, then built dams and ditches
to drain them, turning them into fertile farmlands.
A fleet of steamboats and barges carried Shima's
potatoes from the delta of the Sacramento River
to San Francisco. At the time of his death in 1926,
the "Potato King," as he was called, had an estate
worth $15 million.

Yet success had not protected Shima from racism. When he bought a house in an attractive part
of the city of Berkeley, close to the University of
California campus, a professor led a group of protesters with the message that Shima should move
to an "Oriental" neighborhood. But Shima refused
to move. At Shima's funeral, the chancellor of
Stanford University and the mayor of San Francisco
showed their respect by helping to carry his casket.

An End to Immigration

Many Japanese immigrants believed that their
success, especially in agriculture, would help them
become accepted into American society. They had
failed to recognize the depth of the belief that America was meant to be white. In fact, their very success
as farmers sparked a backlash against them.

In 1907, in an arrangement known as the Gentlemen's Agreement, the federal government had pressured Japan to limit the immigration of laborers to the United States. Six years later California passed the Alien Land Law, which said that no foreigner who was not eligible to become a citizen could buy land. This law was aimed at Japanese immigrants and was based on race. Because the 1790 Naturalization Act said that only "white" persons could become naturalized US citizens, California's Alien Land Law kept the Japanese from buying property in the state.

Takao Ozawa challenged the federal law in 1915 by filing an application for citizenship. He had arrived in the United States twenty years earlier, had graduated from high school and attended college, and had worked and raised a family in Hawaii. When his application for citizenship was turned down, Ozawa fought the decision all the way to the US Supreme Court. In 1922 the Supreme Court ruled against Ozawa, saying that it was clear that he was not Caucasian, or white.

Race-based immigration limits grew tighter by 1924. That year Congress passed a general immigration law that denied entry to any foreigners who were not eligible to become citizens. Neither the Japanese nor any other non-white immigrants could enter the country. A Japanese American newspaper scolded Congress for betraying America's ideals and dishonoring its best traditions. The immigrants' decades of hard work seemed to be for nothing, as reflected in a haiku:

America . . . once
A dream of hope and longing,
Now a life of tears.

Nisei: Americans by Birth

Laws prevented the *Issei*, the Japanese immigrants, from becoming citizens and buying land. Their future in America lay in their children, the *Nisei*, or second generation. The Nisei were a rapidly growing group within the Japanese community. In 1920 more than a quarter of the Japanese population of the mainland United States had been born there. Twenty years later nearly two-thirds of the Japanese population was American-born.

Because they had been born in the United States, the Nisei were citizens. Citizenship together with education, the immigrant generation believed, would give their children opportunities that had been closed to them. Many parents were willing to give up their own comforts, even necessities, for the education of their children.

But citizenship and education, the second generation discovered, did not prevent racial discrimination. Even the Nisei, born in the United States, were called "Japs" and told to "go back to Japan." Japanese American schoolchildren dodged rocks thrown by white children. When they grew a little older they were complimented on their English and asked how long they had been in America.

The Nisei also had trouble finding jobs, even though most of them graduated from high school with good grades and had completed college. The average educational level of the Nisei was two years of college, well above the national average. Still, they were denied opportunities.

Their situation was made worse by the fact that many Nisei came of age during the Great Depression of the 1930s, a time of massive unemployment in the United States. Young people who had dreamed of becoming lawyers or doctors found themselves working in small Japanese businesses such as laundries and fruit stands. A disappointed Nisei who worked in a produce stand explained, "I would much rather it were doctor or lawyer . . . but . . . I am only what I am, a professional carrot washer."

Growing up in America gave the Nisei a sense of twoness, which Monica Sone described in her autobiography *Nisei Daughter*. As a child in Seattle she was surrounded by two cultures. At home she ate traditional Japanese dishes such as pickled radishes and rice, as well as ham and eggs. She studied Japanese *odori* dance as well as ballet.

Monica's family attended Japanese theater, sumo wrestling matches, and picnics where the city's Japanese American community sang the songs and feasted on the foods of their homeland. At the same time, Monica was a member of the Mickey Mouse Club and a kid in American society. While she enjoyed many of her parents' activities, she knew she was not just Japanese.

The biggest problem for Monica and other Nisei was job discrimination. After Monica graduated from high school, she applied to secretarial college and was told that only six Japanese American girls could be admitted, because the school had so much trouble finding jobs for them after they finished their training.

Yet the problem was deeper than employment.

It was a profoundly cultural question: What did it mean to be an American? In their hearts, the Nisei did not wish to be completely assimilated, to become American only. They felt they were a complex combination of two cultures, and they wanted to embrace both of them, to be both Japanese and American.

PICTURE BRIDES

A JAPANESE MAN WHO DREAMED OF GOING TO America could emigrate and enter the United States as a worker. For a Japanese woman, one way to enter America was to marry a Japanese man who was already there—even if she had never met him and had seen him only in a photograph.

The families of men who had emigrated from Japan were eager to find picture brides for their faraway relatives. Picture bride Ai Miyasaki said, "When I told my parents about my desire to go to a foreign land, the story spread through town. From here and there requests for marriage came pouring in just like rain!"

Riyo Orite was also a picture bride. Her marriage to a man in America was arranged through a relative. "All agreed to our marriage, but I didn't get married immediately," she recalled. "I was engaged at the age of sixteen and didn't meet Orite until I was almost eighteen. I had seen him only in a picture at first. . . . Being young, I was unromantic. I just believed that girls should get married. I felt he was a little old, about thirty, but the people around me praised the match. His brother in Tokyo sent me a lot of beautiful pictures [taken in America]. . . .

My name was entered in the Orites' koseki [family register]. Thus we were married."

Marriage is a major life event. So is leaving the land of one's birth to settle in a foreign country. For thousands of Japanese picture brides, the two happened together. Young women crossed the Pacific Ocean and met their husbands the same day they first set foot in their new home, America.

CHAPTER ELEVEN

JEWS ARE PUSHED
FROM RUSSIA

JEWS FROM RUSSIA BEGAN their immigration to
the United States in the 1880s. Like many other
groups, they were pushed into immigrating by
unbearable conditions. But unlike the Chinese
and Japanese workers who had at first planned
to be temporary workers in America, the Russian
Jews came as permanent settlers. They knew there
would be no going back.

Persecution in the Old World

Jews were a persecuted minority in Russia. In an
important sense, those who fled to the United
States were political refugees, because the Russian government itself encouraged acts of violence
against the Jews by the Gentiles, or non-Jews.

Repression was everywhere. Jews were confined
to a special area called the Pale of Settlement in

western Russia. The law prevented them from owning land, forcing most of them to live in urban areas, towns or villages called shtetls. They earned their livings as merchants and craftspeople. In 1879 almost 40 percent of the Jews worked in manufacturing or crafts. This created economic hardships for them, as an immigrant explained:

> It was not easy to live, with such bitter competition as the congestion of the population made inevitable. There were ten times as many stores as there should have been, ten times as many tailors, cobblers, barbers, tinsmiths. A Gentile, if he failed in Polotzk, could go elsewhere, where there was less competition. A Jew could make the circle of the Pale, only to find the same conditions as at home.

Life in the shtetls was intensely insecure. Anti-Semitic violence, or violence aimed at Jews, was a constant reality. Most dreaded were the pogroms, bouts of persecution in which Jews were massacred and their shops and synagogues (temples) destroyed.

"I feel that every cobblestone in Russia is filled

with Jewish blood," an immigrant bitterly recalled. "Absolutely every year, there was a pogrom before Pesach [Passover]. In big cities during the pogroms, they used any reason to get rid of you. As many Jews as they could kill, they did; but there were some Gentiles who would save you."

The pogroms made Jews in Russia and Eastern Europe realize that they had to leave. Many of them looked west, to America.

Dreams of the New World

By the time World War I began in 1914, a third of all the Jews in Russia and Eastern Europe had emigrated. Most went to the United States.

In the old country, the air around them had been full of stories about the freedom and better life they could have in the United States. People read letters from America aloud in shops, markets, and synagogues. Children played games, pretending they were emigrating. America stirred people's hope and dreams of a Promised Land.

Fears of persecution, together with grand visions of a new life, gave the Jews the courage to uproot themselves and leave their birthplace forever. On the streets of the shtetl, women sold their beds, chairs, kitchen tables, and other belongings to raise money for the passage to America. Taking only their personal possessions, the Jews left the familiar little towns of cobbled streets and crowded marketplaces. Like many other emigrants over the centuries, one man realized only at the moment of departure how long his journey would be. "This was the point at which I was cutting myself off from my past, from those I loved," he later recalled. "Would I ever see them again?"

When they boarded ships to cross the Atlantic Ocean, the voyagers were herded into crowded compartments below deck, often dark and dirty. Some emigrants traveled on cattle carriers that had been turned into passenger boats. As often as possible the passengers went up on deck to breathe fresh air. They sang Russian folk songs and shared stories.

Finally, after a long crossing, the passengers sighted land. It was a moment of high emotion. "Everybody was on deck," said Emma Goldman, who was seventeen years old when she arrived from Russia. "[My sister] Helena and I stood pressed to each other, enraptured by the sight of the harbor and the Statue of Liberty suddenly emerging from the mist. Ah, there she was, the symbol of hope, of freedom, of opportunity!"

Who were these newcomers searching for a door to America? In general, they were educated: 80 percent of the men and 63 percent of the women who came between 1908 and 1912 could read and write. Most were poor, but two-thirds of them were skilled workers such as craftspeople. And unlike most other European immigrants, they planned to stay.

Sixty percent of the southern Italian migrants returned to their homeland. For Jews, in comparison, the rate of return was only 3 percent. Another difference was that the Jews immigrated as families. Almost half of them were women, compared to about 20 percent for southern Italians, and a quarter of them were children. They had come to make America their new home.

A Shtetl in America

From the immigration station on Ellis Island in New York Harbor, most of the immigrants headed for New York City's Lower East Side. During the early nineteenth century German Jews had settled in this neighborhood. As massive waves of Russian Jews began arriving in the 1880s, a new Jewish community blossomed there. By 1905 half a million Jews lived in the Lower East Side. Unlike nearby Chinatown, with its high population of single men, the Jewish colony had throngs of children.

In this community, Jews seemed to live the same way they had in Russia. They dwelled and worked within a small area, meeting only people

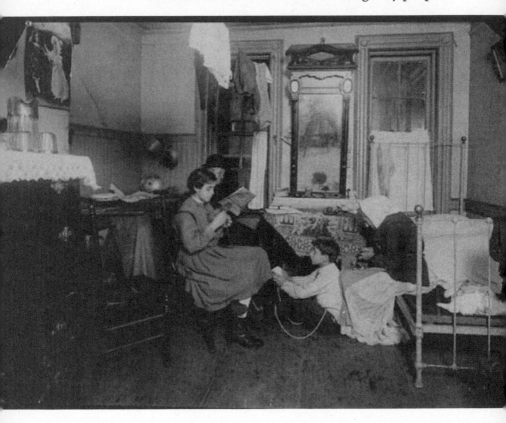

like themselves. Yet life moved at a faster pace, with more emphasis on business, bustle, and making money than in the old country. The atmosphere was one of energy and ambition.

The Jewish neighborhood was also a ghetto, crowded, stifling, and often unsanitary. Residents were packed into six- or seven-story tenement buildings. A typical apartment held not just family members but friends and boarders, too. A survey of two hundred and fifty Lower East Side families in 1908 found that half of them slept in rooms with two or three other people, or even more. Many individuals slept on cots or on the floor.

As they settled in the Lower East Side, the Jews established organizations and created a community of services. *Landsmanshafts* were networks or lodges of people from the same town or district in Russia. Bathhouses, delicatessens, cafés, movie theaters, and synagogues met the immigrants' needs. In the streets, peddlers sold goods such as buttons, bananas, matches, apples, and clothing from carts. The majority of working Jews, however, were employed in the garment industry.

(left) A Lower East Side tenement, New York City, 1912.

An Army of Garment Workers

Jewish success in America depended on more than energy. The Jewish immigrants brought useful skills, especially in the sewing trades. Their arrival was timely, because they were needed in New York City's growing garment industry.

In earlier times, individual pieces of clothing had been tailor-made and measured to fit the buyer, but the Civil War had changed that. To meet the Union Army's demand for clothing, tailors had established standard sizes and measurements. This let them mass-produce clothing in factories using new inventions such as the sewing machine and the buttonhole machine. The number of garment factories increased rapidly, and the center of this new industry was New York City. By 1910 nearly half the city's factories and industrial workers were producing clothing.

At first, German Jews had dominated the garment industry. Then the Russian newcomers entered the business, and together they produced good-quality machine-made clothing that could be sold at moderate prices. The Lower East Side became an industrial beehive, block after block of small, busy workplaces called sweatshops, humming with the sound of thousands of sewing machines.

Most sweatshops were small, with fewer than thirty workers, although some were much larger. They were usually run by contractors who rented the space and equipment and who sold the finished garments to larger manufacturers and distributors. Contractors were paid by the piece of finished clothing, so there was pressure to make as many pieces in as little time as possible.

Laborers worked in teams, with members given specific tasks such as cutting cloth, operating sewing machines, making buttonholes, or pressing the garments. The team received a group wage based on the number of garments they produced, with each member getting a percentage based on his or her task. This system drove everyone to work hard, because each member wanted to speed up the team's pace of production. Performing the same tasks over and over, skilled tailors and seamstresses felt like slaves.

Sweatshop work was physically punishing: hot, noisy, and dangerous. Accidents such as stitching fingers with sewing machines were common. The workday was long, from eleven to fifteen hours. "My work was sewing on buttons," one sweatshop employee said. "While the morning was still dark I walked into a dark basement. And darkness met me when I turned out of the basement."

Daughters of the Colony

Thousands of the garment workers were young women. Many had come to the United States on their own, before their families, because they possessed sewing skills. They could get work, save money, and help the other family members.

These young Jewish women made up more than a third of the garment industry's workforce in 1910. In the sweatshops they were packed together elbow to elbow, operating sewing machines at rows of long tables, so crowded that there was no way to escape in case of emergency.

Disaster struck on March 25, 1911, when a fire suddenly broke out at the Triangle Shirtwaist Company. Eight hundred workers, mostly young women, were trapped in the burning building. Screaming, struggling, they jumped from windows, some from the ninth floor, their bodies smashing onto the sidewalks. Jumping from the higher floors, the girls came down with such force that they tore the nets from the firemen's hands. A hundred and forty-six workers, mostly Jewish and Italian, died. There were so many dead and injured that they could not all be taken away in ambulances and patrol wagons. Grocers and peddlers offered their carts.

Mothers rushed to the scene, where they saw their daughters' blackened bodies laid out on sidewalks. News of the horror rapidly spread to the shtetls of Russia, causing a panic. Families feared that their own daughters or granddaughters or cousins were among the dead.

One reporter wrote, "I looked upon the dead bodies and I remembered these girls were shirtwaist [blouse] makers. I remembered their great strike of last year in which the same girls had demanded more sanitary conditions and more safety precautions in the shops. Their dead bodies were the answer."

The Great Strike

The "great strike" that the reporter mentioned had taken place in 1909–1910, when workers at three factories—including the Triangle Shirtwaist Company—had walked away from their machines and demanded better working conditions. They asked the International Ladies' Garment Workers' Union (ILGWU) to call for a general strike in the entire shirtwaist industry. But the ILGWU had just been founded, and it lacked the resources to organize such a massive strike. The power to do so had to come from the people themselves.

The women strikers organized a mass meeting at Cooper Union, a private college on the Lower East Side. Thousands of people came to show support for the strikers and to criticize the factory bosses—and also the police who were arresting strikers and the hired thugs who were beating them. Inspired by the meeting, the next morning fifteen thousand more shirtwaist workers went on strike. The strike eventually involved twenty thousand workers, overwhelmingly Jewish. Their demands included a fifty-two-hour workweek, overtime pay, and recognition of their union.

During the strike, the Lower East Side was a seething mass of excited demonstrators. Whole neighborhoods burst into applause when word came that another boss had settled with the strikers. By February 1910, more than 300 of the 450 or so shirtwaist businesses in New York had been forced to make some kind of settlement. One was the Triangle Shirtwaist Company. Tragically, although the company agreed to most of the strikers' demands, it did not make safety improvements in time to save the lives of those who perished in the fire a year later.

The Jewish community was proud of its brave and determined strikers, who were commemorated in a poem called "The Uprising of the Twenty-Thousand":

In the black of the winter of nineteen nine,
When we froze and bled on the picket line,
We showed the world that women could fight
And we rose and we won with women's might.

Chorus:
Hail the waistmakers of nineteen nine,
Making their stand on the picket line,
Breaking the power of those who reign,
Pointing the way, smashing the chain.

Several months later another strike erupted when fifty thousand cloak and suit workers walked off their jobs. This strike ended with a compromise between strikers and bosses, in which the strikers received some of the benefits they had demanded.

These labor struggles were a landmark in Jewish American history. They launched a decade of strikes in the garment trades and a period of union growth. "By the end of World War I [1918]," writes labor historian Susan A. Glenn, "clothing workers were among the best-organized members of the American labor force."

The garment strikes were a movement for workers' rights, but they were also an ethnic movement. The great majority of strikers were Jewish, and their struggle held the attention of the Jewish community in America. The labor triumphs sharpened a shared sense of ethnic identity, and in turn Jewish Americans took a continuing interest in the labor movement.

From "Greenhorns" to Americans

When Jewish immigrants arrived in the United States, they were foreigners in their dress, language, and thinking. They called themselves "greenhorns," newcomers who did not yet know their way around. Eager to assimilate into American society, the greenhorns wanted to become modern, to blend in.

To blend in, however, they had to give up certain customs. They had to abandon the clothes they had worn in the shtetls, for example, and dress in the American style: hats instead of caps, collars and neckties for men, bright-colored shirtwaists and jackets for women instead of brown dresses and shawls.

Language was also a mark of assimilation. In

Russia the Jews had spoken their own language, Yiddish. Few of them made any effort to learn the dominant language, Russian. As immigrants in America, though, they were eager to learn English. In a letter to a Jewish newspaper in New York, a mother complained about her daughter: "During the few years she was here without us she became a regular Yankee and forgot how to talk Yiddish. . . . She says it is not nice to talk Yiddish and I am a greenhorn."

The quest to become American led some Jewish immigrants, perhaps many of them, to change their names. Bochlowitz became Buckley, Stepinsky became Stevens. First names changed, too. Rivka became Ruth, Moishe became Morris.

As successful Jews adopted American habits, they celebrated American holidays. To some, exchanging presents at Christmas—which is not a Jewish holiday—was one of the first signs that one was not a greenhorn. Jewish people also began taking vacations, favoring resorts in the Catskill Mountains of New York State. Married women withdrew from the workforce. To have the luxury of not working meant that the wives and their families were economically and socially successful.

Ambition and Education

As unionized workers and businesspeople, the Jewish immigrants acquired the means to educate their children. They were driven by a determination to have the second generation be professionals rather than laborers or merchants.

This determination, however, benefited mostly the sons of the immigrants. Many daughters worked in the sweatshops, contributing their earnings to the family to help pay for their brothers' schooling. In 1910 the income of working daughters amounted to nearly 40 percent of the average Jewish family's earnings.

Meanwhile, young Jewish men were going to the colleges and universities of New York City and other places along the East Coast. By 1916 nearly half the students at New York's Hunter College and almost three-quarters of those at City College were Jewish. Around that time Jews also began to enter Harvard in Massachusetts, which many considered to be the most elite and prestigious college in the country. A fifth of Harvard's student population was Jewish by 1920.

But the increasing presence of Jewish students at Harvard led to a backlash. In 1923 a magazine writer complained that ambitious and upwardly mobile Jewish immigrants sent their children to college a generation or two earlier than other immigrant groups, which meant that there were "more dirty Jews and tactless Jews in college than dirty and tactless Italians, Armenians, or Slovaks." Anti-Semitic grumbles swept across the campus. Some students resented the Jewish students because their grades were so high that they made other students look bad.

Abbott Lowell, president of Harvard, announced that the college had a "Jewish problem." He led efforts to reduce Jewish enrollments. One of his arguments was that keeping the number of Jewish students to a minimum would prevent anti-Semitic feeling on campus.

New admission guidelines at Harvard placed emphasis on "well-rounded" applicants rather than simply on grades, and called for more students from areas other than New York City. Applicants were also required to submit photographs because many people believed it was possible to identify Jews, even if they had changed their names, by their facial features.

Not everyone agreed with Lowell's views. Mayor James Curley of Boston, an Irish American, spoke out against discrimination aimed at Jews. "All of us under the Constitution are guaranteed equality, without regard to race, creed, or color," Curley declared. "If the Jew is barred today, the Italian will be tomorrow, then the Spaniard and the Pole, and at some future date the Irish."

A New Nativism

The anti-Jewish restrictions at Harvard were part of a larger movement of nativism, a way of thinking that favored the established inhabitants of a region or country over newcomers and immigrants, and that placed "native-born" people's interests ahead of the interests of others.

This surge of nativism led to a strict new Immigration Law of 1924 that Congress passed. The law was designed to reduce immigration from southern and eastern Europe. It established quotas, or limits, on the number of people who could enter the United States from each nationality. Each quota was equal to 2 percent of the total number of people of that nationality who had been in the United States in 1890. In other words, the quota system adopted in 1924 was based on population figures that were already more than thirty years old.

Because large-scale Jewish immigration did not occur until after 1890, the number of Jews in America in 1890 was not great—and the number now permitted to enter the country each year was just 2 percent of that number. The same held true for other nationalities. The Chinese Exclusion Act of 1882 had introduced the idea of limiting immigration by nationality. The law of 1924 applied that principle to many immigrant groups, not just one.

The German Jews who had arrived earlier had been welcomed in US society. What made the more recent wave of Russian and Eastern European Jews seem threatening to Americans? They were culturally more different from Americans of English, Scottish, and Irish descent than the German Jews had been. They arrived in much bigger numbers, making people fear an "invasion" of ambitious foreigners who seemed highly successful. In addition, the Russian Jews' involvement in the labor struggle and their participation in strikes seemed threatening.

The more the Jews succeeded, the better they assimilated, the more American nativists disliked them. Hostility sharpened as the Jews began moving out of the Lower East Side, closing the distance between themselves and Gentile America. When

Jews tried to buy homes in more middle-class neighborhoods, they often encountered rules that specified that property could not be sold to Jews. Still, during the 1920s more than a hundred thousand Jews left the Lower East Side, spreading into more distant parts of New York City, such as Brooklyn and the Bronx, and beyond.

Years earlier, as refugees, Jews had fled the shtetls of Russia to what they saw as the Promised Land of America. Now they, or their children, were migrating again, embracing the possibilities of life in the United States, striving to assimilate and become Americans.

COURAGEOUS
CLARA LEMLICH

CLARA LEMLICH WAS A CHILD WHEN SHE
developed a secret reading habit. She was a teenager when she came to America, and she was only
twenty-three years old when she helped lead the
great garment workers' strike of 1909–1910.

Lemlich was born in 1886 in Ukraine, which was
then part of Russia. Her parents would have sent
her to school, but the Russian school did not admit
Jews. They forbade her to speak or read Russian, but
Clara defied her father's orders, learned to read, and
borrowed books whenever she could. She secretly
wrote letters for neighbors to pay for her book habit.
One neighbor's revolutionary pamphlets convinced
her of the need for political and social change.

When Lemlich was seventeen her family emigrated to America to avoid the pogroms. She found
work in a garment shop on the Lower East Side.
Appalled by conditions in the workplace, she got
involved in organizing a union. When the first shirtwaist workers' strikes broke out in 1909, Lemlich
was warned by older male union members—who

considered her a hot-headed pest—that young women could not carry out a large, long-term general strike. She ignored them.

During the historic mass meeting at the Cooper Union, while workers and their families shared their grievances, Lemlich rushed to the platform and insisted on speaking. "I am a working girl," she cried out, "one of those striking against intolerable conditions." Then she said, "I am tired of listening to speakers who talk in generalities. What we are here for is to decide whether or not to strike. I offer a resolution that a general strike be declared—now!" The chairman of the meeting jumped to the platform and joined hands with Lemlich. The two raised their hands high, the crowd pledged to strike, and the next morning twenty thousand workers walked off their jobs.

After the strike Lemlich could not get hired at any New York garment shop. Throughout the rest of her life, in addition to becoming a wife and mother, she fought for women's suffrage, socialism, and the rights of consumers and tenants, and later against nuclear weapons. She died at ninety-six in a Los Angeles nursing home, where she had helped the orderlies organize a labor union of their own.

UNLIKE THE IMMIGRANTS from Asia and Europe, Mexicans lived in a country that bordered the United States. For a long time, entry was easy.

"All you had to do," said Cleofás Calleros, who immigrated with his family from Mexico in the early 1900s, "coming from Mexico, if you were a Mexican citizen, was to report at the immigration office on the American side . . . give your name, the place of your birth, and where you were going to."

Most of the immigrants, however, did not even bother to report to the immigration office. They simply walked across the shallow Rio Grande, and then put on American-style hats and shoes in place of their Mexican sombreros and sandals.

A Pull to the North

Like the Japanese immigrants who arrived at about
the same time, Mexicans saw the United States as
a land of opportunity. They called it *El Norte*, the
North. People who had gone north wrote home to
tell about the good life there, or bragged about it
when they came home to visit. This led more and
more Mexicans to head for El Norte.

"If anyone has any doubt about the volume
of this class of immigrant," wrote an American
reporter in 1914, "a visit to South Texas would
reveal the situation. In a day's journey by automobile through that region one passes hundreds of
Mexicans, all journeying northward on foot, on
burroback and in primitive two-wheeled carts. . . .
When questioned many of them will tell you that
they fled Mexico to escape starvation."

The pull of El Norte was only one force behind
this wave of immigration. Mexicans were also
pushed from their homeland. Large landowners
had been taking over small farms and uprooting
rural families. Forced to become tenant farmers
and sharecroppers, the peasants were exploited in
the countryside, but when they moved to the cities,
they suffered from periods of unemployment as
industries first grew, then shrank.

Poverty was not the only problem. There was
also the danger of violence. The Mexican Revolution began in 1910 and lasted for years, forcing
thousands of refugees to flee northward. One
of them was Jesus Moreno, who arrived in Los
Angeles with his family in 1915. "We came to the
United States to wait out the conclusion of the
Revolution," he said. "We thought it would be over
in a few months."

The movement northward was accelerated by
developments in transportation. In 1895 a railroad
company built a line nine hundred miles into Mexico, linking the Texas border town of Eagle Pass
with the Mexican city of Durango. The railroad
triggered a mass migration. "There is not a day in
which passenger trains do not leave for the border, full of Mexican men who are going in gangs
to work on railroad lines in the United States,"
reported a Mexican newspaper in 1904.

Traveling by train overnight, the men covered a
great cultural distance as well as a great geographi-
cal one. One of their songs told what it felt like to
cross the border by train:

> The fleeting engine
> Can't do anything good

Because at dusk it is at home
And at dawn in a strange country.

Most of the immigrants were from the agricultural labor class, and they were mostly young,
between the ages of fifteen and forty-four. Married men either brought their wives with them or
migrated first and then sent for their families after
they had found work.

Between 1900 and 1930, the Mexican population of the Southwest swelled from an estimated
375,000 to 1,160,00. The majority of these people
had been born in Mexico, not the United States.
They settled in Texas, Arizona, New Mexico, and
California, but some spread out as far as Illinois
and Michigan. Their first concern was to find
work.

Sprinkling the Fields with Sweat

In the early twentieth century, Mexicans were
drawn across the border because the United States
needed their labor. They worked in a wide range
of jobs. Some became urban industrial workers,
serving the construction and railroad industries.
But although three-quarters of the construction

workers in Texas by 1928 were Mexican, they were kept in low-level manual labor jobs. Supervisory and skilled positions were reserved for whites.

In Los Angeles, El Paso, and other cities with a large Mexican population, the majority of Mexicans worked in garment factories, canneries, or food-processing plants, or as janitors and gardeners, not in banks and offices. A federal official explained why a Mexican made a good railroad worker: "His strongest point with his employers is his willingness to work for a low wage."

Most Mexicans, however, worked in agriculture. In California, farmers turned to Mexican labor after immigration laws ended the flow of workers from Asia. At least two-thirds of the state's two hundred thousand farm laborers in the 1920s were Mexican. In Texas, the percentage was even higher. The state employment service estimated that 85 percent of Texas's agricultural laborers were Mexican. Many of them were hired for the backbreaking work of picking cotton all day under the hot Texas sun.

Farm work was seasonal and migratory. Packed into old trucks and cars, laborers followed the crops. Their location at any given time was determined by where the jobs were. An immigrant named Anastacio Torres recalled picking cotton in

California in 1919, then, when the cotton season ended, working in a paper plant in Los Angeles, and after that returning to agricultural work in the Imperial Valley, where he picked lemons.

The migrant laborers lived in squalid camps with crude shelters, often made of canvas or even palm fronds. The growers felt no responsibility for the health or comfort of their workers. One farmer bluntly stated, "[When] they have finished harvesting my crops, I shall kick them out on the country road. My obligation is ended."

Mexicans on Strike

Feeling that they were entitled to dignity as well as better working conditions and higher wages, Mexicans took part in labor struggles, especially during the Great Depression of the 1930s. Between 1928 and 1933, Mexican farm laborers in California had had their wages cut from 35 to 14 cents an hour. In response, they supported strikes led by a variety of labor unions.

By actively participating in the labor movement, Mexicans challenged the stereotyped image of people from their country as passive and easygoing. Growers reacted with alarm to the formation of Mexican unions, and to their militancy.

One of the most powerful Mexican strikes occurred in 1933. Twelve thousand laborers in the San Joaquin Valley struck to resist cuts in their pay. To break the strike, growers kicked the workers out of their camps, dumped their possessions on the highway, and used the local police to arrest strike leaders. A deputy sheriff told an interviewer: "We protect our farmers here in Kern County. They are our best people. . . . But the Mexicans are trash. They have no standard of living. We herd them like pigs."

The Mexican strikers refused to back down. Women were especially active. They came to the picket lines every day, and they called out to strikebreakers, urging them to join the strike. A worker named Lydia Ramos explained why she would not cross the picket lines as a strikebreaker: "Well, we believe in justice. So I want everything that's good for me and I want everything that's good for somebody else. Not just for them . . . but equality and justice." In the end, the strikers reached a compromise with the growers and received a wage increase.

The strikes represented a deep discontent with life in El Norte. One of the strikers, Juan Berzunzolo, had come to the United States in 1908 and worked on the tracks of the Southern Pacific railway and in the beet fields of Colorado. "I have left the best of my life and strength here," he said, "sprinkling with the sweat of my brow the fields and the factories of these gringos [Anglos]."

Tortillas and Turbans

Working in the fields alongside the Mexicans were immigrants from India. At the beginning of the twentieth century, workers from the Punjab, a region of northern India, started arriving on the West Coast of the United States. By 1920 some 6,400 had entered the country. Nearly all of them were men, and most of them were Sikhs, members of a religion that had originated in India in the sixteenth century. They wore turbans, a piece of cloth wrapped around their heads.

The Sikhs had been farmers in the Punjab, so they gravitated toward farm labor in America. Like the Mexicans, the Sikhs followed the harvests of different crops. Sikh men and Mexican women met each other while working in the fields and orchards. They formed relationships that sometimes led to marriage.

Love was not the only reason for Sikh men to

marry Mexican women. Sikhs were not considered white by American courts. Therefore they could not become naturalized citizens. The Alien Land Law of 1913 said that foreigners who were not able to become citizens could not buy land. Sikhs could, however, acquire land through their Mexican wives if they bought it in their wives' names.

"Two years ago I married a Mexican woman," said Inder Singh, a Sikh farmer in the Imperial Valley in 1924, "and through her I am able to secure land for farming. Your land law can't get rid of me now; I am going to stay."

In Sikh Mexican families, two cultural traditions met and blended. Foods were interchanged—Mexican tortillas and the flat Indian breads called rotis; jalapeño peppers and Punjabi chillis. Languages were mixed as well. Mexican wives usually understood some Punjabi, but English and Spanish were spoken in the home, and the Punjabi fathers learned to speak Spanish with their children. In most cases the children were baptized as Catholics, like their Mexican mothers, and raised under the *compadrazgo* (godparents) system of the Catholic Church and the Spanish culture.

The number of Sikh Mexican marriages was not large. Still, these couples—and the families they produced—added one more flavor to the multicultural mix of American society.

On the Other Side of theTracks

Mexican laborers were allowed to be in the United States as laborers, but they were kept from becoming full members of society. They could shop in Anglo parts of town only on Saturdays, and they could get food in Anglo cafés only by sitting at the counter or taking their food out. Mexicans lived in segregated neighborhoods called barrios. In many towns the barrios were located on the other side of the railroad tracks from where the Anglos lived.

Schools were segregated, too. One educator said, "There would be a revolution in the community if the Mexicans wanted to come to the white schools. It is based on racial inferiority." In their segregated schools, young Mexican Americans were trained to become obedient workers. Like the Hawaiian sugar planters who wanted to keep the American-born generation of Japanese on the plantations, Anglo farmers in Texas wanted the schools to help reproduce the labor force. The sugar-beet growers worried that if every Mexican got a high-school education, there would be no one to pick their beets.

"Educated Mexicans," one farmer said, "are the hardest to handle. . . . They make more desirable citizens if they would stop about the seventh grade." One Mexican American student remembered his sixth-grade teacher advising him not to go to high school, with these words: "Your people are here to dig ditches, to do pick and shovel work. I don't think any of you should plan to go to high school."

Some teachers, though, gave Mexican American children a sense of dignity and self-respect. In his autobiography *Barrio Boy*, Ernesto Galarza fondly recalled his school principal and teachers who never punished children for speaking Spanish on the playground. "Becoming a proud American," Galarza said, "did not mean feeling ashamed of being a Mexican."

Beginning in the 1920s, Mexicans found that they were no longer wanted in the United States. Nativists had grown alarmed at the large number of Mexican immigrants. Referring to the mixed-race background of many Mexicans, one nativist said: "From the racial point of view, it is not logical to limit the number of Europeans while we throw the country open without limitation to Negroes, Indians, and half-breeds."

Magazines and newspapers published hysterical articles about the "Mexicanization" of the United States. Anglo workers spoke out against the Mexicans who competed with them for jobs, and the American Federation of Labor, one of the country's labor unions, complained about the use of Mexicans as cheap labor, which was putting white men out of work.

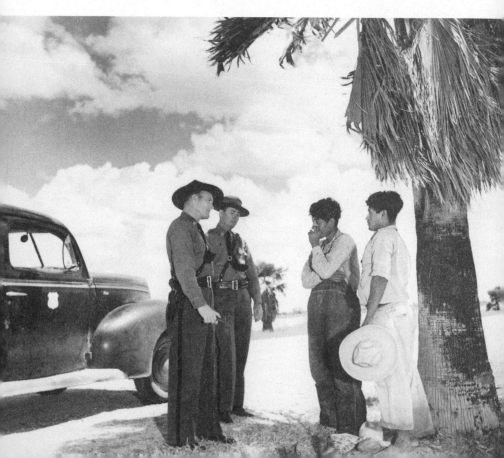

Then came the Great Depression of the 1930s. Unemployment skyrocketed. Thrown out of work, and blamed for the loss of white workers' jobs, Mexicans became targets of a program called repatriation, which meant returning them to their country of origin. In fact it was deportation—forcing people to leave the country they were living in.

Private charities and government agencies used a variety of tactics to encourage Mexicans to go back to Mexico. They threatened to cut off welfare aid, they offered free transportation by train (which sometimes meant being crammed into a boxcar), and they used police raids to pressure people into leaving or, in some cases, to physically remove them.

Some four hundred thousand Mexicans were sent out of the country during repatriation. Many were children. The Los Angeles Chamber of Commerce estimated that about 60 percent of those children had been born in the United States and were US citizens.

The Barrio: A Mexican American World

For many Mexicans, the border was only an imaginary line between Mexico and the United

(left) United States border patrol officers question Mexican workers, 1940.

States—one that could be crossed and recrossed at will. Living in El Norte, they created a Mexican American world called the barrio.

Barrios were ethnic islands. There Mexican Americans did not feel like strangers, as they did when they ventured across the railroad tracks into Anglo parts of town.

Barrios were often slums, made up of shacks and dilapidated houses without sidewalks or even paved streets, but Mexicans could celebrate their national holidays there, eat the familiar foods of home, tell stories about Mexico, and play their traditional music in bands that displayed both the US and Mexican flags.

What bound the people of the barrios together was not just their Mexican ethnicity but also their economic class. Everyone was poor, and everyone was looking for work. The barrios were networks of job information. They also served as places where new arrivals from Mexico could sleep, eat, and learn the ropes of life in America. People shared what they had, not as charity but as *asisten-cia*, help that was given and received on trust, with the idea that those who were helped would repay the kindness someday.

As evening fell on the barrios, people sat in

front of their houses and talked, just as they had done in villages on the other side of the border. They spoke of their love for their homeland, and they complained about racism and discrimination in the United States. Yet despite their nostalgia and their complaints, most of them stayed. They were making El Norte their homeland.

Although the word barrio was first used in the United States to describe these Mexican American communities, mostly in the West, these were not the only centers of Latino life and culture in America. In many cities across the country, Spanish-speaking communities formed, made up of immigrants not just from Mexico but from Central and South America and the Caribbean as well. One of the largest of these communities is Spanish Harlem, also known as El Barrio or East Harlem—a neighborhood in northeastern Manhattan, in New York City, that became home to Puerto Rican migrants as early as the 1920s. It has a large population of Nuyoricans, who are second- and third-generation Puerto Ricans, born in the United States.

KICKED OUT OF
THE COUNTRY

SIX-YEAR-OLD IGNACIO PIÑA AND HIS FAMILY
were in Hamilton, Montana, in 1931. His father and
oldest sister were out in the sugar-beet fields one
day, and his mother was cooking tortillas, when
authorities suddenly burst into their home with
guns and told them to get out. The family was not
allowed to take anything with them—not even the
trunk that contained the birth certificates of Ignacio and his five siblings, proof that all six of them
had been born in the United States and were US
citizens.

The Piña family was thrown into jail for ten
days, then put on a train and sent to Mexico. They
were just one of many families uprooted during
the repatriation movement of the 1930s, when US
authorities used bullying, trickery, and threats to
ship up to four hundred thousand Mexicans and
Mexican Americans to Mexico. Like Ignacio Piña,
many of the deportees were children who were US
citizens. Repatriation means "returning to one's
homeland," but these children had never been to
Mexico. They had been born in the United States,

and repatriation violated their legal right to be in the country.

For the Piñas, repatriation was a disaster. The whole family became ill with typhoid fever. Ignacio's father died four years later. "My mother was left destitute, with six of us, in a country we knew nothing about," says Piña. "We were misfits there. We weren't welcome."

In the slums of Mexico City, Piña's education went only as far as the sixth grade. Still, sixteen years after he was deported, he managed to get the documents he needed to prove that he had been born in Utah. He returned to the United States, worked for a railroad, and made sure that his children went to college. Decades after repatriation, though, the painful memories remained fresh. "The Depression was very bad here. You can imagine how bad it was in Mexico," he said. "You can't put 16 years of pure hell out of your mind."

MEXICANS TREKKING TO EL NORTE were not the only people who migrated northward in the early twentieth century. Southern blacks were moving by the tens of thousands to the cities of the Northeast and the Midwest. The spirit behind this migration was later described by Zora Neale Hurston, an African American writer who was a sharecropper's daughter:

And Black men's feet learned roads. Some said good bye cheerfully . . . others fearfully, with terrors of unknown dangers in their mouths . . . others in their eagerness for distance said nothing. The daybreak found them gone. The wind said North. Trains said North. The tides and tongues said North, and men moved like the great herds before the glaciers.

(left, detail) The Renaissance Casino ballroom in Harlem, New York City, 1927.

In just ten years, from 1910 to 1920, the black population jumped from 5,700 to 40,800 in Detroit, from 8,400 to 34,400 in Cleveland, from 44,000 to 109,400 in Chicago, and from 91,700 to 152,400 in New York. The African Americans who made this journey were both pushed from the South and pulled to the North.

Pushed and Pulled

Like the immigrants from Asia, Mexico, and Europe, southern blacks were driven from their homes by economic and social forces. After the abolition of slavery and the emancipation of the slaves, most blacks in the South had been forced to become sharecroppers and tenant farmers. They were dependent on white landowners and enslaved all over again, this time by debt.

The ordeal of sharecropping was crushing. After months of labor, at the end of the harvest season tenant farmers were often disappointed to find themselves deeper in debt. They were politically free but in economic bondage, with no hope of getting ahead and owning their own land:

Where I come from
folks work hard
all their lives
until they die
and never own no part
of earth nor sky.

Meanwhile, they were pulled to the North. World War I, which had begun in Europe in 1914, had cut off the flow of European immigrants into the United States. This created tremendous labor shortages in the nation's industries. Factories, mills, and workshops that had once refused to hire black workers now sent labor recruiters to the South to sign them up.

Southern blacks jumped at this opportunity. Whole trainloads of them set out for the North, drawn by the offer of better work and better wages. One black worker told a reporter, "The best wages I could make [in Georgia] was $1.25 or $1.50 a day. I went to work at a dye house in Newark, N.J., at $2.75 a day, with a rent-free room to live in. The company paid my fare North."

Like Mexican immigrants, African Americans were following the jobs. Those who went North sent home glowing reports about work. A South

Carolina newspaper described the good fortune of a young man from a Greenwood County farm who had gone north to work for twenty-five dollars a week: "He came home last week to assist his people on the farm and brought more than one hundred dollars and plenty of nice clothes. He gave his mother fifty dollars, and put fifty dollars in the Greenwood bank and had some pocket change left."

But something more was happening among blacks in the South, something that went deeper than economics. The generation that had been freed from slavery was dying out, and so were the habits that slavery had bred into that generation: habits of giving way to whites, of accepting their "place" in society. Southern whites lamented that the humble, polite, and courteous blacks they had known were disappearing. In their place a new generation of blacks was rising.

The New Generation

In place of the old-time former slaves, the South now had younger African Americans who had been born after the Civil War and had never known slavery. Unlike the older generation, this new generation did not feel the lingering power of the master-slave relationship. Whites complained that the younger blacks were "discontented and wanted to be roaming." They wanted to see something of the world.

Most of the blacks who moved North belonged to the generations that arose after the Civil War. In addition to the higher wages they expected to earn in the North, these African Americans also hoped to escape the racial violence and prejudice of the South, to find a place where they could claim some dignity. A black-owned newspaper called the *Chicago Defender* spelled out the need for African Americans to come north for the sake of their safety and self-respect:

> *Why stay in the South, where your mother, sister and daughter are raped and burned at the stake; where your father, brother and sons are treated with contempt and hung to a pole, riddled with bullets at the least mention that he does not like the way he is treated?*

Freed from the shadow of slavery, young blacks could imagine new possibilities for themselves in the North. By 1930, about two million of them had migrated to the cities of the North. Their freedom had been given to them by the North in the Civil War, but their migration was their own choice.

African American Chicago

Chicago was a major destination of the African American blacks. The fast-growing industries of this midwestern city were creating jobs and actively inviting blacks to fill them. It was easy for southern blacks to get to Chicago, too. The Illinois Central Railroad connected the city to the small towns of Mississippi, Arkansas, and Louisiana.

In 1900, Chicago's black population numbered 30,000. Twenty years later, it had jumped to 109,000, concentrated in the mostly black neighborhoods of the city's South Side. This rapid increase in the black population sparked an explosion of white resistance.

White citizens formed organizations to pressure real estate agents not to sell houses to blacks. They also urged white property owners not to sell or rent to blacks. A leader of this movement declared, "The districts which are now white must remain white. There will be no compromise."

The conflict over housing increased during World War I as blacks flocked to fill jobs in Chicago's war-related industries. In 1917 the Chicago Real Estate Board announced that southern blacks were "pouring into Chicago at the rate of ten thousand a month."

Workplaces also became racial battlegrounds. In 1910 about half of all working blacks were employed in service jobs: servants, laundresses, janitors, and waiters. The war created a sharp demand for labor and opened new opportunities in industry. By 1920 the majority of black men and 15 percent of black women worked at factory jobs rather than service jobs. For the first time in their lives, these young African American men and women were working in industries and making what they considered good wages.

Managers deliberately hired black workers to undermine the union activities of white workers. Company owners hired a black man named Richard Parker to set up a black union, the American Unity Labor Union. Although Parker appeared to be working to promote African American interests, in reality he was paid by the white business owners to pit black workers against whites, so that blacks would not join the white union. It was the old strategy of divide and control again. By keeping black and white workers from uniting, management kept both groups from reaching their full strength.

Parker urged black workers not to trust the whites and to sign up only with the black union. The strategy worked. When a white union called the Stockyards Labor Council opened the door to black members, its offer was rejected.

Racial tension in the workplace added fuel to conflicts in the neighborhoods. In 1917 the homes of several black families were bombed. White gangs attacked blacks in the streets and parks, murdering several men. Race hatred exploded into a riot after a young black man drowned when he floated into the "whites only" section of a public beach. Frustrated because the police made no arrest, blacks attacked whites. White gangs then began beating blacks, and violence between the races raged for days. By the time the rioting ended, twenty-three blacks and fifteen whites were dead, and 342 blacks and 178 whites were injured.

African Americans in Chicago responded to racism by depending on themselves. Black ministers and community leaders called for people to start their own shops, banks, and insurance companies.

Blacks, they said, should rent from other blacks and spend their dollars on goods made and sold by African Americans.

Black Pride in Harlem

The other major destination of the African American migrants was New York City, home of Harlem, a neighborhood that was sometimes called the "Negro Capital of the World."

Blacks had lived in Harlem since the seventeenth century, when they were the slaves of Dutch colonists in North America. In 1790, not long after the United States won its independence, a third of Harlem's population was black. Over the years, though, the African American presence there grew smaller. By 1890 Harlem was a wealthy, mostly white neighborhood—and then the black migration from the South changed it again.

Just as the migration started, a housing boom in Harlem collapsed, leaving a large number of apartments empty. Black real estate agents leased these apartments from the white landlords and then rented them to black tenants at a profit. In this way Harlem began to become a black neighborhood again, in spite of residents who tried to keep African Americans out, just as they had done in Chicago.

In 1914 about 50,000 blacks lived in Harlem. During the 1920s more than 118,000 whites left the neighborhood, and more than 87,000 blacks moved in. Harlem had become the home of more than two-thirds of all the African Americans who lived in Manhattan.

Soon, however, Harlem was overcrowded. Living conditions grew worse as landlords neglected the upkeep of their properties. Tenants complained about broken pipes, leaking roofs, and rats. Yet discrimination made it difficult for blacks to move to other parts of the city, so they were

forced to remain in Harlem, paying higher and higher rents.

High rents were a burden to African American tenants because most of them worked in low-paying menial or service jobs. Some black women worked in the garment industry, but the majority was employed as domestic servants. Some men were longshoremen or teamsters, but many were janitors, elevator operators, and waiters.

Despite crowded living conditions and poor wages, African Americans in Harlem felt a surge of power and a sense of pride. They were inspired to create a community that became more than just a place to live. To black intellectuals, Harlem became what poet Langston Hughes called the center of the "New Negro Renaissance."

Black poets like Hughes, novelists like Jean Toomer, painters like Jacob Lawrence, and musicians like Cab Calloway were attracted to Harlem, a community that reflected a vision of black pride and creativity. Drawing their inspiration from black people's lives, history, and culture, Harlem's black intellectuals created a literature that rebelled against mainstream, white-dominated, middle-class America.

Part of the New Negro movement was the search for identity that Hughes revealed in his

(left)
The Renaissance Casino ballroom in Harlem, New York City, 1927.

poetry. He asked whether he belonged to Africa or to "Chicago and Kansas City and Broadway and Harlem." Like other African Americans, he was struggling to create a sense of himself that was both African and American.

The Great Depression

By the late 1920s, Harlem had become a slum, the home of poor people desperately clinging to dreams. The Harlem Renaissance, with its cabarets, its swinging jazz, and its literary successes, hid much of the ghetto's squalor. Then came the stock market crash of 1929, followed by the Great Depression that lingered for most of a decade. The shattering of the economy revealed the grim reality behind the glamorous image of Harlem.

African Americans everywhere fell into deeper poverty. Despite the great migration to the North, most American blacks still lived in the South in the 1930s, growing cotton as tenant farmers and sharecroppers for white farmers. Their livelihoods crumpled along with the stock market. When blacks moved to cities in search of work, they were met by angry out-of-work whites shouting against the hiring of African Americans.

By 1932 more than half of all blacks in southern cities were unemployed. The unemployment rate for blacks in northern cities was similar. Black employees were the first to be fired when times got tough. One study found that the proportion of unemployed blacks was 30 to 60 percent greater than that of whites. Many desperate families, unable to afford apartments or groceries, lived in cellars and foraged in garbage cans for food.

Federal aid programs for people in distress forced African Americans to take a backseat. White farmers and workers received higher rates of support than blacks. This crisis led to debate among black Americans about their future.

W. E. B. Du Bois, the nation's leading black historian and scholar and a leader in the National Association for the Advancement of Colored People (NAACP), had long pushed for integration, an end to racial separation. During the hardship of the Great Depression, however, he suggested that African Americans should practice voluntary, temporary segregation, banding together and helping one another, doing business only with one another, forming a black nation within the United States. The NAACP harshly criticized this idea, calling instead for a movement that would "unite all labor, white and black, skilled and unskilled, agricultural and industrial."

Blacks had indeed begun to enter industrial employment and the big national labor unions. In 1933 the United Mine Workers led a campaign to bring black workers into the union, and the Committee for Industrial Organization (CIO) soon did the same. In the auto industry, the United Auto Workers urged blacks to join, pledging that the union was against racial discrimination. These achievements did not mean the end of racism among white workers, but they showed that solidarity across racial lines was essential for workers who were struggling against management in a time of economic crisis.

Meanwhile, Democratic politicians recognized the size and potential power of the black vote. They began addressing the needs of blacks. In response, blacks started to abandon the Republican Party—the party of Abraham Lincoln, who had freed the slaves—in favor of the Democratic Party. Black Americans were becoming politically important, but their advances in labor and politics were soon swept up, along with much else, in the international currents of World War II.

THE AMBITIOUS ARCHITECT OF BLACK PRIDE

IF ONE PERSON EMBODIED THE VISION OF BLACK pride that swept through Harlem like a fresh wind, it was Marcus Garvey. "Up, you mighty race," he declared to blacks in America, "you can accomplish what you will."

Born on the Caribbean island of Jamaica, Garvey experienced a childhood free of racial awareness. "To me, at home in my early days, there was no difference between white and black," he later wrote. Garvey and a white friend played together without thinking about their skin color—until Garvey was fourteen, when his friend's parents separated them because of Garvey's race.

"It was then," Garvey wrote, "that I found for the first time that there was some difference in humanity, and that there were different races, each having its own separate and distinct social life." A few years later Garvey traveled to Europe, where he began to develop ideas about Black Nationalism— a sense of devotion to black culture, along with a belief that blacks should express unity, pride, and power. In 1914 he returned to Jamaica and founded the Universal Negro Improvement Association (UNIA) to promote Black Nationalism, with the goal of uniting the black people of the world and establishing an African American nation in Africa.

Garvey's message was that black skin is beautiful, that Africa had a glorious past, and that blacks were destined to rule Africa. "If Europe is for the Europeans, then Africa shall be for the black peoples of the world . . . ," he wrote. "The other races have countries of their own and it is time for the 400,000,000 Negroes to claim Africa for themselves."

In 1916, Garvey made Harlem the base of his movement. The UNIA exploded with activity: colorful parades, publications, the establishment of black-owned small businesses such as groceries and laundries, and even the founding of a shipping company called the Black Star Line in which African Americans could invest.

The Black Star Line was the biggest symbol of the UNIA, but it was badly managed and ran into debt. In 1922 Garvey was charged with defrauding investors, even though the government's case was weak and there was no proof that Garvey had intended to commit fraud. Sentenced to five years in prison, Garvey was pardoned after two and deported to Jamaica.

But although Garvey was gone, the powerful dreams he represented remained alive in the hearts of the people of Harlem and blacks everywhere. By strengthening their sense of racial pride, he had forever changed the way black people looked at themselves. *The Spokesman*, an African American publication, declared, "Garvey made thousands think, who had never thought before. Thousands who merely dreamed dreams, now see visions."

CHAPTER FOURTEEN

WORLD WAR II AND AMERICA'S ETHNIC PROBLEM

WORLD WAR II BEGAN IN EUROPE in 1939 and later spread to the Pacific Ocean. The United States did not join the fighting until after Japan bombed the US naval base at Pearl Harbor, Hawaii, on December 7, 1941. Then the nation mobilized for war. Soon, US troops were seeing combat around the world.

The war pitted two groups of countries, the Allies and the Axis, against each other. The Allies were the United Kingdom, France, and many other countries, including the United States. The three main Axis powers were Germany (controlled by Adolf Hitler's Nazi party) and Italy in Europe, and Japan in Asia and the Pacific.

The Nazis claimed that white people of Germanic descent were a "master race." They were superior to others, including Jews, who were

(left, detail)
"V for victory," New York City, 1945.

targeted for Nazi persecution, along with Gypsies, Catholics, homosexuals, and other groups whom the Nazis considered inferior. Nazi beliefs were a form of fascism, a political viewpoint that defines nationhood in terms of a unified, dominant, shared culture and ancestry. Fascism sees the world in terms of "us" and "them"—with "them" as inferiors, outsiders, or weaklings.

The racist underpinnings of Nazism and fascism led some people to question how the United States could battle these repulsive ideas in other countries while racism remained alive in America. World War II forced Americans to take a critical look at the racial and ethnic divisions within their own society. Minorities experienced the war differently, but their experiences, taken together, showed that World War II was not just a fight for equality and democracy abroad. It was also the beginning of new stage in the struggle at home.

Japanese Americans: A Hole in the Constitution

One result of the Japanese attack on Pearl Harbor was fear and suspicion directed at Japanese people living in Hawaii and on the U.S. mainland—including Japanese Americans who were US citizens.

In the days immediately after the bombing, federal authorities arrested a total of fewer than 2,100 Japanese, German, and Italian people in the United States who were believed to be dangerous to US security. But when the military and President Franklin D. Roosevelt debated rounding up everyone in the country who was of German, Italian, or Japanese descent, the president decided that the Germans and Italians were not a problem. What about the Japanese?

The secretary of the Navy wanted people of Japanese descent living in Hawaii to be interned, or rounded up and confined under guard. Lt. General Delos Emmons, the military governor of Hawaii, disagreed. "There is no intention or desire on the part of the federal authorities to operate mass concentration camps," he told the people of Hawaii. "While we have been subjected to a serious attack by a ruthless and treacherous enemy, we must remember that this is America and we must do things the American Way." For Emmons, the "American Way" meant respecting and enforcing the US Constitution.

Although Roosevelt approved a plan to remove

twenty thousand "dangerous" Japanese from Hawaii, Emmons ordered the internment of only 1,444 people who posed a possible threat. Emmons also pointed out that no known acts of sabotage had been committed in Hawaii.

The fate of the 120,000 Japanese Americans living on the West Coast was far different. J. Edgar Hoover, the head of the Federal Bureau of Investigation, said that there was no security reason to intern them. Francis Biddle, the attorney general of the United States, declared that interning them would be racist and would "make a tremendous hole in our constitutional system." In spite of these arguments, Lt. General John L. DeWitt, the military commander of the West Coast, had no confidence that people of Japanese ancestry would be loyal to the United States, even if they were US citizens. The president left the decision up to the military, and DeWitt ordered all people of Japanese ancestry on the West Coast to be forcibly relocated to guarded camps.

Japanese and Japanese American residents, taking only what they could carry of clothing and household supplies, had to abandon their homes, possessions, and businesses, many of which were snapped up at bargain prices by white buyers. The

Japanese were loaded into trains and sent off to unknown destinations: hastily built camps, mostly located in remote desert areas. There the internees were crowded into barracks, with whole families sharing a single room. Barbed-wire fences and guard towers became the horizons of their strange and humiliating new life.

The few Japanese who resisted being interned were arrested and convicted. Although they fought their convictions all the way to the US Supreme Court, they were told that the singling out of the Japanese was a military necessity, although there was no evidence that this was true.

American-born Japanese men were, however, allowed out of the camps in order to enlist in the US armed services. Thirty-three thousand of them enlisted. They believed that helping to defend their country was the best way to prove their loyalty and fulfill their duties as citizens.

Several thousand Japanese Americans served as translators and interpreters in the Pacific. To carry out their missions, they sometimes crawled close enough to Japanese officers in the middle of battle to hear commands so that they could translate for their American comrades. One high-ranking intelligence officer estimated that these contributions by Japanese Americans shortened the war by two years.

Japanese Americans also served in Europe. The 442nd Regimental Combat Team, made up of Japanese Americans from the mainland and Hawaii, won great distinction in a series of bloody battles in Italy and France. Members of the 442nd earned more than 18,000 decorations, including more than 3,600 Purple Hearts.

Yet upon returning from the war with missing limbs and chests covered with military medals for heroism, Japanese American soldiers could still be turned away from barbershops with the words, "We don't serve Japs here." And when the internment camps closed and families traveled by train back to the cities where they had lived before the war, they were greeted with signs saying, "No Japs allowed, no Japs welcome." For many of the internees, release from the camps meant starting over, for their homes and livelihoods had been lost.

African Americans: Racism in the Armed Forces

Some nine hundred thousand African Americans enlisted in the US armed services during World

War II. They served, however, in a segregated military. They were confined to black-only regiments and training camps. They were prevented from using the churches and clubs on military bases. Often they were given the lowliest assignments, such as cooking and cleaning, or the most dangerous ones, such as handling explosives and munitions.

When given the chance, African Americans seized opportunities to prove themselves in combat. The nation's first black military aircraft pilots, trained at Tuskegee Air Force Base, earned respect in the bullet-torn skies over France and Germany, where they served as protectors of white pilots. The African American 761st Tank Battalion stood its ground in the Battle of the Bulge, one of the fiercest campaigns in the European theater of war. Black women served in the Women's Army Corps in Europe, processing mail and working side by side with white WACs.

Blacks across America were stunned and angered by President Roosevelt's refusal to end racial segregation in the armed services. Many accused the government of hypocrisy, saying one thing but doing the opposite. The United States claimed to be fighting for freedom and democracy—but it did so with a "Jim Crow army," one that was officially segregated by race.

African Americans did, however, win one victory during the war. In the summer of 1941 Roosevelt signed an executive order that banned racial or ethnic discrimination in employment for government or defense jobs.

Threats of a large African American protest march may have influenced Roosevelt. The real pressure for integration in the defense industries, though, came from the need for labor in the steel mills, shipbuilding yards, aircraft plants, and munitions factories that built America's war machines. With manpower pulled into the armed services, these industries desperately needed labor. They began to hire more black men, and they also hired women, both white and black. A million African Americans were employed in defense industries during the war. More than half were women.

But as African Americans followed defense jobs into the cities, they often found themselves targeted by hate crimes and violence. Competition between blacks and whites existed in the workplace. Conflict also arose over living space in the crowded city, because blacks had to live in segregated ghettos. In 1943, in the middle of the war, racial tensions in Detroit grew so extreme that fierce rioting broke out and lasted for three days, leaving twenty-five blacks and nine whites dead.

President Roosevelt did not speak out against the racial violence in Detroit, but a group of wounded American soldiers did. They wrote from their hospital to a newspaper in their home city of Detroit, saying that the riot made them ask what they were fighting for. They declared they were fighting, and were willing to die, for the "principles that gave birth to the United States of America." They signed the letter: "Jim Stanley, Negro; Joe Wakamatsu, Japanese; Eng Yu, Chinese; John Brennan, Irish; Paul Colosi, Italian; Don Holzheimer, German; Joe Wojiechowski, Polish; and Mike Cohen, Jewish."

Their names with their ethnic identities said it all: the war for freedom still needed to be won at home.

Chinese Americans:
An Explosion of Patriotism

America's entry into the war set off patriotic outbursts in Chinatowns across the country. In New York City's Chinatown, excited crowds cheered themselves hoarse when the first men drafted into the army were Chinese American.

Chinese Americans wanted to enlist in the armed forces in order to gain respect. "To men of my generation," explained Charlie Leong of San Francisco, "World War II was the most important historic event of our times. For the first time we felt we could make it in American society."

The war gave Chinese American men the opportunity to get out of Chinatown, wear army uniforms, and be sent overseas, where they felt they were part of a great patriotic American force. One soldier recalled, "In the 1940s for the first time Chinese were accepted by Americans as being friends, because at that time, Chinese and Americans were fighting against the Japanese and the Germans and the Nazis. Therefore, all of a sudden, we became part of an American dream."

A total of 13,499 Chinese Americans—more than one-fifth of the adult Chinese American men in the country—were drafted or enlisted in the armed forces during World War II. In civilian life, meanwhile, Chinese American workers found new opportunities. For decades they had been limited to an ethnic labor market with most jobs in restaurants and laundries, but the wartime need for labor opened up higher-paying jobs, especially in defense industries. In Los Angeles, for example, three hundred laundry workers closed their shops to help build the ship *China Victory*. Chinese American workers also found employment in aircraft plants.

Women moved into new areas of employment along with the men. Many held office jobs, but in 1943 a Chinese American newspaper reported on Alice Yick, a mechanic trainee in the Boston Navy Yard, as well as on the first Chinese American women to work in California's aircraft industry, building B-24 bombers.

World War II also brought changes to government policies toward Chinese immigration. Anti-American radio broadcasts from Japan highlighted racist treatment of Chinese people in the United States and the US laws that limited Chinese immigration and prevented Asian immigrants from becoming citizens. This led Congress to repeal the Chinese Exclusion Act that had kept Chinese people from entering the country. Instead, Congress set a quota for Chinese immigration. It was a tiny trickle—just 105 people a year—but Chinese Americans had won an important victory. Under the new law, they could also become naturalized citizens.

Mexican Americans: Up from the Barrio

A twenty-seven-year-old Mexican American named Alex Romandia was working as a stuntman in Hollywood when he heard the news of the Japanese attack on Pearl Harbor. Together with several Jewish friends, Romandia volunteered for the army. "All of us had to prove ourselves," he said, "to show that we were more American than the Anglos."

Half a million Mexican Americans enlisted in the armed services—almost one-fifth of the group's total population of 2,690,000. Many saw their service as a way to show that although they held strong ties to their Mexican heritage, the United States was their country.

Mexican Americans suffered high casualty rates and won many distinctions. One of them, Guy Louis Gabaldon, received a military award for a unique achievement. Growing up in the barrio of East Los Angeles, he had become friendly with a Japanese family, from whom he learned Japanese. When the war started, the family was sent to an internment camp.

Gabaldon, seventeen years old, joined the marines and was sent to the Pacific. During his first day of combat on the island of Saipan, he killed thirty-three soldiers. Filled with remorse, he decided he would try to persuade the remaining Japanese to surrender, because they were surrounded and cut off from the Japanese navy. Working alone, he captured six Japanese soldiers, then told them that he would shoot three of them if the other three did not bring more soldiers back to him. Within seven hours, Gabaldon had eight hundred prisoners.

Mexicans also made important contributions on the home front. To meet the need for farm labor, the federal government started a program in which guest workers, called braceros, could enter the country from Mexico to work for a specific period of time. By 1947 about two hundred thousand braceros had worked in the United States.

Like blacks, many urban Mexican Americans—both men and women—worked in defense industries. Between 1941 and 1944 the number of Mexican Americans employed in the Los Angeles shipyards rose from zero to 17,000. Thousands of Mexican American women became riveters, learning how to drill and assemble aircraft parts.

For many Mexican Americans, defense jobs were both an expression of patriotism and a chance for personal growth. On the job, people learned work skills and social skills. They gained confidence and broadened their horizons. Antonia Molina, who worked at a defense plant, recalled a lesson in tolerance:

> I remember one day when some new Black workers came to our factory. From the start, some white workers absolutely refused to even say hello. The next day, some of us Mexican women invited the Black women over to our table for lunch. We did so because we knew what it was like to be discriminated against. By the end of the week, several white workers also joined us for lunch. We soon realized that we had to set aside our differences in order to win the war.

Native Americans: Why Fight the White Man's War?

When war came, young Indians wondered why they should fight in "the white man's war." Why enlist in the US armed services, when Native Americans had been losing their land ever since the first English colonizers landed at Jamestown in 1607?

Yet many Native Americans did join the fight. Enlistment was especially high among the Navajo people. Almost one-fifth of all the Indians who came from reservations to enlist in World War II were Navajo.

Patriotism and pride led Indians to enlist. When asked why Navajo joined the services, Raymond Nakai replied, "Our answer is that we are proud to be American. We're proud to be American Indians. We always stand ready when our country needs us."

Another reason was poverty. By the time of World War II, the federal government's program to reduce the number of livestock on the Navajo reservation had made the Indians poor and dependent on wages. The Navajo had an average annual income of $128, two-fifths of which came from wages, mostly from temporary government work. Young men saw military service as a way of improving their lives.

More important, the Navajo possessed a unique skill that made them desirable to the military. "The marines recruited Navajo for our language," said Cozy Stanley Brown. "They like to use our language in war to carry messages."

Navajo who were fluent in both English and their

tribal language could be trained as "code talkers." The Japanese military could not understand or mimic the Navajo language, because the sounds of many words could be heard only by native speakers, and verb forms were so complex that only someone who had grown up with the language could use them properly. The US military admiringly called the Navajo language an "unbreakable code."

In February 1945 the Navajo code talkers took part in one of the most important Pacific battles: the fight for the island of Iwo Jima. During the first two days of the US invasion of Iwo Jima the code talkers worked around the clock, sending more than eight hundred messages without error. Four code talkers were killed in the fighting. Major Howard Conner declared, "Without the Navajos, the marines would never have taken Iwo Jima."

After the war, however, Navajo and other Native Americans returned to their reservations bearing physical and psychological scars from their war experiences. They also found that economic conditions there had not improved. A year after the war, the average man on the Navajo reservation was earning less than $100 a year.

Many Navajo saw the irony of being valued for their tribal language—a language that the government had tried to keep them from using. "When I was going to boarding school," said Teddy Draper Sr., "the U.S. government told us not to speak Navajo, but during the war, they wanted us to speak it!"

Jewish Americans: Facing Genocide

When Hitler came to power in Germany in 1933, four and a half million Jews were living in the United States. They were safe from Nazism, but they faced an agonizing problem. How should they respond to events in Europe? Germany's anti-Semitism and persecution of Jews became, during World War II, genocide—an organized plan to destroy a particular people.

During the 1930s, as the situation for German Jews steadily worsened, the majority of Americans opposed relaxing the immigration quota so that more German Jews could immigrate into the United States. According to one poll, 66 percent of Americans did not want the government to let in even Jewish children who were at risk in their home country.

After President Roosevelt and the US government turned away the *St. Louis*, a ship carrying more than nine hundred German Jews who had fled from Nazi Germany, American Jews felt a deep sense of frustration. They had been loyal citizens. Many of them, as well as prominent Jewish American organizations, had said at first that the United States should not make exceptions to the immigration laws. But once it became clear that a ghastly fate awaited Jews in Germany, calls to admit them into the United States as refugees grew louder.

In 1942, the year after the United States entered the war, news of Hitler's concentration camps, massacres, and plans to eliminate the "Jewish problem" through mass murder reached the US government and Jewish American leaders. Even then, the president declared that the only way to aid the Jews of Europe was to win the war. He was unwilling to admit them to the country as refugees.

Finally, in 1944, Roosevelt appointed a War Refugee Board to plan the rescue of victims of the Axis powers. The rescued victims were to be housed in North Africa. Only one thousand could come to the United States. Meanwhile, at Auschwitz, one of the major Nazi death camps, twelve thousand were being killed each day. By the time Allied forces defeated Germany in June 1945 and liberated the camps, six million Jews had been exterminated in a genocide that has come to be known as the Holocaust.

One result of the Holocaust was that Jewish Americans became more strongly committed to Zionism, a movement to give the Jewish people their own homeland. Membership in the Zionist Organization of America jumped from 18,000 in 1929 to 52,000 in 1939, and then to 136,000 in 1945.

In 1947 the General Assembly of the United Nations voted on a plan to divide the Middle Eastern nation of Palestine into two states, one Arab and the other Jewish. The Jewish state, Israel, would be the Jews' new homeland. The following year President Harry Truman signed a document recognizing the new country of Israel.

A Holocaust Called Hiroshima

Truman had been Roosevelt's vice president. He became president in 1945, when Roosevelt died suddenly. He was the leader of the United States when World War II ended a few months later.

Like many Americans, Truman had been swept into a revenge-seeking rage by the treacherous attack on Pearl Harbor. The violent conflict in the Pacific was a war of racial hatreds. The American military and media portrayed the Japanese enemy as subhuman and bestial. Truman shared this view. In diary entries written in 1945, the president expressed hatred for the "Japs—savages, ruthless and fanatic." He was determined that the only acceptable outcome of the Pacific war was Japan's complete and unconditional surrender.

In 1945 Truman gained a tool powerful enough to bring about that surrender. The Manhattan Project, a scientific and military mission to develop an atomic bomb, had been successfully completed. When Japan refused Truman's order for unconditional surrender, the United States dropped two bombs— the only two atomic bombs ever used in warfare—on the Japanese cities of Hiroshima and of Nagasaki.

After two cities and hundreds of thousands of people had been instantly incinerated, Japan agreed to surrender, on one condition—that it is allowed to keep its emperor. Truman, who did not want to drop a third bomb, agreed. The war was finally over.

World War II ended in victory for the United States and its allies. For minorities in America, however, the fight against prejudice still had to be won. In the words of African American historian W. E. B. Du Bois, the war was a struggle "for democracy not only for white folks but for yellow, brown, and black."

DOUBLE V FOR VICTORY

WEEKS AFTER THE UNITED STATES ENTERED
World War II, a young African American man in
Kansas inspired a movement that swept the nation,
encouraging black people to fight for democracy at
home as well as overseas.

James G. Thompson, age twenty-six, worked
in the cafeteria of a factory that manufactured
aircraft for the war. On January 31, 1942, an African American newspaper called the *Pittsburgh
Courier* published a letter he wrote called "Should
I Sacrifice to Live 'Half American'?" This is what
Thompson wrote:

> *DEAR EDITOR:*
> *Like all true Americans, my greatest desire*
> *at this time, this crucial point of our history;*
> *is a desire for a complete victory over the*
> *forces of evil, which threaten our existence*
> *today. Behind that desire is also a desire to*
> *serve, this, my country, in the most advanta-*
> *geous way. Most of our leaders are suggesting*
> *that we sacrifice every other ambition to the*

paramount one, victory. With this I agree; but I also wonder if another victory could not be achieved at the same time. . . .

Being an American of dark complexion and some 26 years, these questions flash through my mind: "Should I sacrifice my life to live half American?" "Will things be better for the next generation in the peace to follow?" "Would it be demanding too much to demand full citizenship rights in exchange for the sacrificing of my life?" "Is the kind of America I know worth defending?" "Will America be a true and pure democracy after this war?" "Will colored Americans suffer still the indignities that have been heaped upon them in the past?". . . .

The "V for Victory" sign is being displayed prominently in all so-called democratic countries which are fighting for victory over aggression, slavery and tyranny. If this V sign means that to those now engaged in this great conflict then let colored Americans adopt the double VV for a double victory . . . The first V for victory over our enemies from without, the second V for victory over our enemies within. For surely those who perpetrate these ugly prejudices here are seeing to

destroy our democratic form of government
just as surely as the Axis forces. . . .
  In way of an answer to the foregoing
questions in a preceding paragraph, I might
say that there is no doubt that this country
is worth defending; things will be different
for the next generation; colored Americans
will come into their own, and America will
eventually become the true democracy it was
designed to be. These things will become a

(above)
White Americans
celebrate one of
the victories, New
York, 1945.

reality in time; but not through any relaxation of the efforts to secure them.

In conclusion let me say that though these questions often permeate my mind, I love America and am willing to die for the America I know will someday become a reality.

JAMES G. THOMPSON

The *Courier* turned Thompson's idea into the Double V campaign. The Double V went on to be featured in dozens of articles, not just in the *Courier* but in other black papers as well. Double V clubs and pins helped promote the belief that African Americans, who were fighting in foreign lands to defend democracy, deserved complete equality in their own country.

CHAPTER FIFTEEN

CALLS FOR CHANGE

AMERICA'S RACIAL, ETHNIC, and religious minorities had helped fight the country's enemies in Europe and the Pacific during World War II. Now they faced a different battle at home: the battle against discrimination. Out of the war came calls for change. In the decades after the war, a cascade of presidential decisions and new laws changed conditions for America's racial and ethnic minorities, moving the nation closer to social justice for all.

One of the first changes took place in 1948. Three years after the war ended, the US armed services were still segregated by race. That was unacceptable to a black civil rights activist and labor leader named A. Philip Randolph, who had been calling for an end to discrimination in the military.

Randolph met with President Harry Truman to push for equal rights and equal treatment for blacks and whites in the nation's military. Pointing out the unfairness of letting blacks fight without granting them equality, Randolph declared, "Negroes are in no mood to shoulder guns for democracy abroad, while they are denied democracy here at home." Facing the possibility of a large protest march by African Americans, Truman issued an executive order requiring equal treatment and opportunity for everyone in the armed services.

Japanese Americans Raise their Voices

Like other Japanese who were living in California before the World War II, Kajiro and Kohide Oyama had spent the war as prisoners in one of the US government's internment camps.

When the Oyamas were released from the camp, they returned to California and asked the courts to overturn the state's Alien Land Law of 1913, which prevented them from owning property in their own names because, as non-white immigrants, they could not become citizens. The Oyamas had owned land in the name of their young American-born citizen son, but while the Oyama family was being held in the internment camp, the state had tried to seize the property.

The Oyamas took their case all the way to the US Supreme Court. In 1948 the Court decided that California had acted illegally in trying to take over the Oyamas' land. Justice Frank Murphy described California's Alien Land Law as "outright racial discrimination." This paved the way for California's state supreme court to declare the Alien Land Law unconstitutional in 1952.

By that time the United States had passed another major milestone in its multicultural history. In 1952, under pressure from lobbying groups that included Japanese American war veterans, Congress did away with the part of the Naturalization Act of 1790 that said only "white" immigrants could become US citizens. Now immigrants of any skin color could seek citizenship.

By 1965, about 46,000 Japanese immigrants had taken their citizenship oaths. Many were elderly and had lived in the United States as noncitizens for decades. One of them, Kioka Nieda, rejoiced in poetry:

> *Going steadily to study English,*
> *Even through the rain at night,*
> *I thus attain,*
> *Late in life,*
> *American citizenship.*

For Japanese Americans, one more ghost still had to be laid to rest—the memory of the mass internment during World War II. For years many Japanese Americans carried that burden in silence. By the 1970s, however, the third generation wanted to break the silence. They asked their elders to tell them of their experiences during the war, and they organized pilgrimages to the camps.

Japanese Americans began asking for congressional hearings to make their voices heard. As a result of the hearings, in 1988 Congress passed a bill that officially apologized for the internments and awarded $20,000 to each survivor. When President Ronald Reagan signed the bill into law, he admitted that the US government had committed a serious wrong. Reagan pointed out that Japanese Americans had remained "utterly loyal" during the war and called the internment "a sad chapter in American history."

Protest in the Barrios

The winds of protest also swept through the nation's Mexican American neighborhoods, or barrios. After the war, Hispanics felt more than ever stung by discrimination when restaurants, stores, and other businesses refused to serve them on an equal basis with white customers. "We knew this was totally unfair," said Juana Caudillo, who had spent the war years in a job related to national defense, "because we had worked hard to win the war."

Mexican Americans who had served in the war were determined to be victorious over discrimination at home. They founded a civil rights organization called the GI Forum in Corpus Christi, Texas, in 1948. Membership grew rapidly. Within a year the GI Forum had more than a hundred chapters in twenty-three states. In addition to organizing a boycott of a company that discriminated against Hispanics in employment, members of the GI Forum called for bilingual education, with classes taught in both English and Spanish.

The war had changed Mexican Americans, turning some into activists. When a veteran named Cesar Chavez returned from the battle against fascism, he dedicated himself to the struggle of farm workers. His mission was to combat prejudice and win decent wages for Mexican American agricultural laborers, the people who picked the nation's crops of grapes and lettuce in California and many other states.

Women shared the Mexican American desire for change. As one of them explained:

> *When our young men came home from the war, they didn't want to be treated as second-class citizens any more. We women didn't want to turn the clock back either regarding the social positions of women before the war. The war had provided us the unique chance to be socially and economically independent, and we didn't want to give up this experience simply because the war ended. We, too, wanted to be first-class citizens in our communities.*

Determined to fight discrimination, Mexican Americans wanted to end the practice of segregated education, which meant putting students of different races into separate schools or classrooms. In 1946, in the case of *Mendez v. Westminster School District of Orange County,* the US Circuit Court of Southern California ruled that segregating Mexican children in school violated their right to equal protection under the law, as guaranteed by the Fourteenth Amendment to the US Constitution. This victory went beyond the Mexican

American community. It led California to repeal
a law under which school districts had segregated
Chinese, Japanese, and Indian children.

The Civil Rights Movement Begins

The *Mendez* case paved the way for a historic
US Supreme Court decision in 1954. In the case
known as *Brown v. Board of Education*, the court
ruled that racial separation in schools was unconstitutional. The decision applied to all public
schools in the nation. Segregation, or racial separation, would be replaced by integration, the mixing
of races on an equal footing.

The National Association for the Advancement
of Colored People (NAACP) had presented the
argument against segregation to the Supreme
Court justices. The group greeted the ruling as
a victory for all of the American people, and as
a sign that the United States deserved to be the
leader of the free world. Thurgood Marshall, a lawyer for the NAACP who later became a Supreme
Court justice himself, had been certain that after
the bravery and patriotism that African American
and Japanese American soldiers had shown in
World War II, Americans would have to respect

the country's black and Asian citizens as the equals of whites.

But although the Supreme Court had made racial integration in schools the law of the land, integration remained largely a court ruling on paper. Years would pass before the nation's school districts would put it fully into action. In the meantime, pressure for change would come not from the courts but from a people's movement for civil rights.

That movement was born in 1955 in Montgomery, Alabama, when an African American woman named Rosa Parks refused to give up her seat on a city bus to a white man. She was arrested. Parks was not the first African American to challenge segregation on public buses in the South. Others, including teenagers, were also protesting discrimination in this way. Parks's arrest, however, triggered a large protest: a boycott in which the city's black population refused to ride the buses.

A young black minister named Martin Luther King, Jr. organized the protest. King had seen that although about half of the residents of Montgomery were black, most were limited to working as domestic servants or common laborers, and all were walled in by segregation in schools and on buses. His inspiring leadership of the bus boycott helped make him a leader in the civil rights movement that was taking shape across the South.

"I Have a Dream"

The civil rights movement challenged segregation through direct action. Confrontations occurred in Greensboro, North Carolina, when black students sat at a drugstore lunch counter that had a "whites only" policy. Under the leadership of a group called the Student Nonviolent Coordinating Committee (SNCC), similar sit-ins took place in dozens of cities and towns.

These actions did not just end segregation at lunch counters. They brought an enormous growth in pride and self-respect among the young people who participated. "I myself desegregated a lunch counter, not somebody else, not some big man, some powerful man, but me, little me," said one black student. "I walked the picket line and I sat in and the walls of segregation crumbled. Now all people can eat there."

"Freedom rides" soon followed, organized by the Congress of Racial Equality (CORE). In these acts of civil disobedience, black and white civil rights supporters defiantly rode together in buses into

Southern bus terminals. There they were sometimes yanked from the buses and brutally beaten by racist white mobs in front of television cameras. Medgar Evers, the leading black civil rights activist in Mississippi, was murdered in 1963.

The summer of that year brought the famous March on Washington. Two hundred thousand people gathered in the nation's capital to demand equality for all. The crowd massed near the Lincoln Memorial, which honored the president who had delivered the Gettysburg Address a century earlier, and who had freed the slaves with his Emancipation Proclamation. There Martin Luther King, Jr. spoke to the marchers, the nation, and the world, sharing his vision of freedom in America:

Five score years ago, a great American, in whose symbolic shadow we stand, signed the Emancipation Proclamation. . . ., I say to you today, my friends, that in spite of the difficulties and frustrations of the moment, I still have a dream. It is a dream deeply rooted in the American dream. . . . I have a dream that one day this nation will rise up and live out the true meaning of its creed: "We hold these truths to be self-evident: that all men are created equal. . . .

(left) Sit-in at a whites-only lunch counter in St. Petersburg, Florida, around 1960.

Blacks and Jews

Joachim Prinz also spoke at the March on Washington. Prinz was a rabbi—a leader of a Jewish congregation—who had survived the death camps of Nazi Germany. He told the crowd that the most urgent problem of racial injustice was not hatred or prejudice. It was silence. Onlookers who wit-

ness injustice and do nothing, Prinz warned, are morally guilty, for they allow injustice to continue.

Prinz's presence at the March on Washington showed the alliance that existed between African Americans and Jews in a civil rights movement that was racially mixed. Marchers and protesters sang, "Black and white together, we shall overcome someday," and indeed, whites were involved in the movement. More than half of them were Jews. In addition to taking part in events such as the freedom rides, Jewish civil rights supporters provided financial aid and legal services to the NAACP, SNCC, CORE, and King's Southern Christian Leadership Conference. Three civil rights workers working to register black voters were murdered in Mississippi in the summer of 1964. James Chaney was African American; Andrew Goodman and Michael Schwerner were Jewish American.

Some Jewish Americans joined the crusade for justice for African Americans because they remembered the persecution and violence they or their parents had experienced in Russia. They saw that racism and anti-Semitism were much alike, and that both blacks and Jews had much to gain by ending discrimination.

The black-Jewish alliance fell apart, however,

(left) Freedom riders make a test trip into Mississippi, 1961.

when the focus of the civil rights movement shifted from the lunch counters and bus stations of the South to the cities of the North. Economic and class divisions existed between Jews and northern urban blacks.

Jews owned about 30 percent of the stores in black communities such as Harlem in New York City and Watts in Los Angeles. During race riots, blacks looted those stores along with others. Many ghetto blacks also noticed that their landlords were Jewish, and they questioned whether blacks could work with Jews when Jewish property owners were exploiting black tenants.

At a deeper level, the split between African and Jewish Americans reflected differing visions of equality. The civil rights movement had begun as a struggle for black equality through integration. Success meant equal treatment for the races, first at schools, lunch counters, and bus stations, then in equal opportunity for voting and jobs.

Starting in the mid-1960s, though, young militant blacks like Stokely Carmichael and Malcolm X raised the call of Black Power. They believed that blacks, united by race, should determine their own fate. There was no place for whites, including Jews, in this movement for black liberation.

But the civil rights movement, made up of blacks and whites together, had won important victories. In 1964 and 1965, Congress passed laws and President Lyndon Johnson signed executive orders that outlawed discrimination in public accommodations (such as hotels and buses); established a commission to promote equal employment opportunity; removed obstacles such as literacy tests that were designed to prevent blacks from voting; and required companies that worked for the federal government to make special efforts to hire minorities. The result of these changes was a different America, one in which discrimination was no longer woven into law and habit.

Economic Inequality

The civil rights movement, however, could not overcome all of the problems faced by African Americans. Laws and court orders could end discrimination, but they could not end poverty. African Americans had won the right to sit at a lunch counter and order a hamburger—but many did not have the money to do it. And while the law now made it illegal for employers to show racial discrimination in hiring, salaries, or promotions, blacks saw that jobs for them were scarce.

Riots in Watts in 1965 highlighted the anger and frustration that many blacks felt. Malcolm X, born Malcolm Little, expressed this frustration when, after firsthand experience of ghetto life, drugs, crime, and prison, he said, "I don't see any American dream. I see an American nightmare."

The nightmare continued, and so did the violence. Malcolm X was assassinated in 1965, two years after President Kennedy was slain by an assassin's bullet. Race riots exploded throughout the late 1960s in cities such as Detroit, Chicago, and Newark. The year 1968 brought two more shocking assassinations: Martin Luther King, Jr., the foremost symbol of the civil rights movement, and Robert F. Kennedy (brother of the president), who as attorney general of the United States had been a strong supporter of civil rights. Bombings were also carried out in the late 1960s and early 1970s by a group called the SDS (Students for a Democratic Society), a violent offshoot of the student antiwar and civil rights movements.

Meanwhile, the civil rights movement had hit the walls of an inequality that was based on economics as well as on race. Beginning in the 1960s, black America became deeply splintered into two classes. The middle class experienced gains in education and income, while the "underclass" was mired in poverty and unemployment.

Plants and offices had migrated to the suburbs, putting jobs out of reach for many urban blacks. Factories closed as manufacturing jobs were moved offshore to other countries. This further reduced employment opportunities for black workers, who had been heavily concentrated in the automobile, rubber, and steel industries. Many of the jobs that remained available were low-wage service jobs, such as working in fast-food restaurants, that led nowhere.

Economic inequality made America's inner cities into explosive places. One of the worst explosions erupted in Los Angeles in April of 1992, after four white police officers who had violently beaten a black man named Rodney King were found not guilty of the charges against them. Racial rage engulfed the city. Thousands of fires burned out of control, looting was widespread, and losses totaled $800 million.

Out of the fires, however, came an awareness of multicultural connectedness. Social critic Richard Rodriguez said, "The Rodney King riots were appropriately multicultural in this multicultural capital of America."

Pointing out that the riots revealed tension between African Americans and Korean store owners, and that many of the looters who had been arrested were Hispanic, Rodriguez concluded, "Here was a race riot that had no border, a race riot without nationality. And, for the first time, everyone in the city realized—if only in fear—that they were related to one another."

In 2008 the United States reached another multicultural milestone when, for the first time, the American people elected a nonwhite president: Barack Hussein Obama, the Hawaiian-born son of a white American mother and a black father from the African nation of Kenya. In spite of this sign of progress, race remained a thorny issue in national life, and economic inequality continued to plague a larger share of blacks than whites. At the same time, an economic downturn for the nation and the world meant shrinking opportunities for millions of people of all races.

TEENAGERS STAND UP (AND SIT DOWN) FOR FREEDOM

YOUNG PEOPLE WERE VITAL TO THE CIVIL RIGHTS movement in the South. For some black students in Montgomery, Alabama, in the 1960s, after-school activities included protesting against racial injustice—and getting arrested for it.

A young minister named Martin Luther King, Jr. had helped organize the Montgomery Improvement Association (MIA) in 1955 to protest segregated seating for blacks on the city's buses. The MIA won that fight in 1956 when the city obeyed a court order requiring racial integration on the buses, but the larger battle for equal treatment in all parts of life continued. Gladis Williams was one of many young activists who protested the unequal treatment of blacks and whites in the city's stores and lunch counters.

"We would go after school to the MIA office, and we would organize," she said. "First of all we would find out who was going to what store. Girl/boy, girl/boy. Nobody went by themselves. We would always have a mixed group. We'd get the names, telephones, addresses of next of kin for the different people who were going."

Once at the stores, Gladis and the other kids sometimes marched outside with protest signs and sometimes went in to sit at the "Whites Only" lunch counters. "Don't even ask me how many times I was arrested!" Williams said. "They arrested us for unlawful assembly and for demonstrating without a permit. They would get us for disorderly conduct, or disturbing the peace, even though we were very orderly."

Going to jail was, for Williams and the other activists, "a badge of honor at that time. When you demonstrated, you already knew it's possible you're going to jail. It's possible you're gonna get hurt. It's possible you're gonna get killed. . . . So far as having fear, we didn't even know what fear was. We just had our minds set on freedom, and that was it."

CHAPTER SIXTEEN

NEW WAVES OF
NEWCOMERS

THE WORLD HAS CONTINUED to rush into America, weaving more threads into the nation's complex multicultural tapestry. The civil rights movement of the 1960s focused on race relations within the United States. Meanwhile, during the movement and after, new waves of foreigners kept immigrating. Some of these newcomers came from familiar shores, such as China. Others, such as the immigrants from the Caribbean, Vietnam, and Afghanistan, opened new links between their homelands and America.

As always, many of the newcomers have been pushed from their homelands by war, poverty, and political or religious persecution. At the same time, they have been pulled to America by the dream of freedom and an economic fresh start.

The Door Opens to the Chinese

In the 1960s, as the United States passed new civil rights laws to address the problem of discrimination against blacks, some Americans questioned the immigration law, which still assigned quotas based on national origin. Under the quota system, only a set number of people from each country could enter the United States every year. In many cases, such as China, Japan, and the countries of black Africa, "national origin" really meant "racial origin." In fact the immigration law discriminated not just by nationality but by race as well. Lawmakers began to call for an end to this system.

"Just as we sought to end discrimination in our land through the Civil Rights Act," said one congressman, "today we seek by phasing out the national origins quota system to eliminate discrimination in immigration to this nation composed of the descendants of immigrants." In 1965 Congress responded by removing all restrictions on Asian immigration—an injustice that Asian Americans had tried for decades to overcome.

For the Chinese, the new law reopened the gates to the land they had once called Gold Mountain. In 1960 there were 237,000 Chinese in the United States. By 1980 the number had jumped to 812,200. Before the new wave of immigration, the majority of the American Chinese population had been born in the United States. Afterward, the majority was foreign-born.

Chinese students flocked to the United States for education. By 1980 half of the three hundred thousand foreign students in the country were from China or other Asian countries. Many of them were able to find jobs as skilled workers, which let them exchange their student visas for immigration papers. At that point they could bring their wives and children to the United States. Once they became US citizens, they could bring their parents and siblings as well. In this way one Chinese student could set in motion a chain migration of family members.

Not all of the new Chinese immigrants were educated. Many spoke English poorly or not at all. Their employment opportunities were limited. Like generations of immigrant women before them, a large number of the new Chinese female immigrants found jobs in the garment industry. Often they worked for minimum wages in sweat-shop conditions. A Chinatown resident said in the mid-1980s, "The conditions in the factories are terrible. Dirty air, long hours, from eight in the morning to eight at night, six days! They are paid by the piece and only a few can make good money. They don't protest because they don't know how to talk back and they don't know the law."

Some of the immigrants, though, were well educated and had held professional jobs in China. Even these immigrants found it hard to obtain good jobs in America. One couple had been an architect and a biology professor in China. Unable to speak English, they toiled at low-paying menial jobs until a federal program called the Comprehensive Employment Training Act provided funds for the wife to take English classes and begin a new career in library science, and became the head librarian in UC Berkeley's Asian American Library. Like the earlier immigrants from China, the new wave wanted to assimilate and succeed, but they had to overcome steep challenges to do so.

Vietnamese War Refugees

Unlike the immigrants from China, the Vietnamese were war refugees who were fleeing for their lives. From 1955 to 1975 their homeland had been torn by the Vietnam War, a civil conflict in which the United States supported South Vietnam while communist North Vietnam received aid from China.

The war ended disastrously for South Vietnam and the United States. The South Vietnamese government collapsed, and North Vietnamese troops marched into the capital of the south. Just before the government fell, ten to fifteen thousand Vietnamese people were evacuated from South Vietnam. Most were military personnel who had been US allies, and their families.

Then, in the frenzied last days before the North Vietnamese arrived, another eighty-six thousand fled from the country. From the roof of the American embassy they climbed into helicopters. Most had no chance to prepare for emigration—they had less than ten hours' notice that they would be leaving. Many thought they would be gone for only a month or two.

A total of about one hundred thirty thousand Vietnamese refugees found sanctuary in the United States in 1975. They came from the educated classes, and they generally had some familiarity with Western customs. About two-thirds of them spoke English well. After entering the United States through processing stations on military bases, they were spread throughout the country, but they soon began to gather and form ethnic communities in places like Orange County, California.

Meanwhile, life in Vietnam under a new communist government, in the aftermath of a massively destructive war, was brutally difficult. People were marched into the countryside and forced to dig canals and do farm work. As one immigrant recalled, "Life was very hard for everybody. All had changed! I could see no future for me in Vietnam, no better life! I wanted to escape."

Thousands did escape in this second wave of departures—more than 277,000 by 1979. They took their families aboard crowded, leaky boats, braving the dangers of storms and pirates to sail to ports in Thailand, where they waited in refugee camps to be sent to Australia, Canada, France, and especially the United States. Many of them were ethnically Chinese, people who had lived in Vietnam and experienced discrimination there. Unlike the first wave of Vietnamese refugees, the second wave generally did not speak English.

By 1985 there were 643,200 Vietnamese living in the United States. "Remember these are people who were on our side," said an American veteran of the Vietnam War. "They have a right to come to

322

this country as refugees. They just need a home." Still, like earlier Asian immigrants, the Vietnamese did not feel welcome, and they felt the sting of racial slurs.

In their adopted country, many refugees realized that they could not completely maintain their traditional Vietnamese culture, especially where gender roles were concerned. In America, Vietnamese women became wage earners and gained new independence. Family relationships became strained when college-educated young women who wanted professional careers tried to break away from the traditions of arranged marriage and female obedience. As the younger generation spoke English more often, some felt their Vietnamese language slipping away.

Over the years, as the refugees had children and made places for themselves in American society, they began to realize that their stay in the United States would be permanent. By 2000 their numbers had increased to about 1.4 million. They formed ethnic colonies, many of them in California, where 40 percent of Vietnamese Americans live. As the Vietnamese entered medicine, business, retail trade, and other professions, they added a new element to American multicultural-ism. In turn, they were transformed, becoming no longer purely Vietnamese but rather Vietnamese Americans.

Terrorism and Afghan Refugees

Like the Vietnamese, the Afghans came to the United States as refugees, but from a different war and a different region of the world. Afghanistan, their homeland, is a landlocked Muslim country about the size of Texas, located in South Asia.

Afghanistan became a battleground in the Cold War, the conflict between the United States and the communist world that dominated international politics after World War II. The Cold War ended in 1991 when the Soviet Union, a communist superpower made up of Russia and neighboring countries, broke up.

Twelve years before the Soviet Union went out of existence, it invaded Afghanistan. To prevent the Soviets from gaining control there, the United States helped finance and train anti-Soviet militias. Meanwhile, a number of Afghans fled to the United States as political exiles and refugees.

The fighting lasted ten years, but in 1989 Soviet troops withdrew from Afghanistan in defeat. Before the exiled Afghans could return home, however, civil war broke out among various factions within their country. In 1996 a fiercely conservative, anti-Western faction called the Taliban seized control of Kabul, the Afghan capital. Refugee Sediqullah Rahi said, "The Taliban are primitive, closed-minded people. They are not allowing anything progressive in Afghanistan. Our economy is destroyed, our social life is destroyed, our people's lives are nothing." Refugees who had thought of returning to Afghanistan put their plans on hold.

Then came 9/11—the fateful day of September 11, 2001, when Muslim hijackers attacked the World Trade Center towers in New York and the Pentagon in Washington, DC. The terrorists were traced to Al-Qaeda, an underground organization based in Afghanistan. The following year, the United States and a group of other nations invaded Afghanistan.

Afghans in the United States lived not only with bitter memories of fleeing from their homeland but also with worry about what the Taliban was doing to their country and its people. Then, after 9/11, they also faced anti-Muslim hostility in the United States. As soon as news of the attacks

appeared on television and the Internet, Afghan Americans began to fear for their safety. "It was at this moment that I realized everything is going to change," recalled one of them in 2007. "Being Afghan American is not what people think it was before; now it's what people want to know about you and who you really are inside, an American or a terrorist."

Some Afghans pretended they were Mexican, Greek, or Italian to prevent abuse. Others demonstrated their American loyalties by hanging US flags on their homes and businesses. A young woman named Fatema Nourzaie, who had been born in California after her parents fled from Afghanistan, told how 9/11 affected the Muslim community in the United States: "I started hearing how girls in hijab (Muslim women's scarves) were being attacked. Indians were getting shot because they 'looked' Middle Eastern, and mosques were getting burned down. That was the only time I ever was afraid to be a Muslim."

Even before that world-shattering event, Nourzaie had struggled over what it meant to be Afghan American. "I don't think I could ever label myself completely as one or the other," she said. "I am just as much American as I am Afghan."

(left) Pakistani neighborhood near Newkirk Avenue in Brooklyn, New York, 2005.

In her view, Afghan Americans are an example of successful integration, not assimilation, because they have kept their culture and identity rather than losing it in mainstream America. "Afghans have kept their uniqueness, the beauty of their culture, and at the same time have thoroughly functioned in today's society. I think that's what integration means."

Afghan Americans are part of a larger population subgroup in the United States, made up of people of South Asian descent, from Bangladesh, India, and Pakistan as well as from Afghanistan. During the 1990s, South Asians became one of the fastest-growing parts of the American population. The great majority of South Asians in the United States are of Indian descent. The 2010 census recorded 2.6 million Indian Americans, making them the nation's second-largest group of Asian Americans, after the 3.2 million Chinese Americans.

Crossing the Border to El Norte

By the early twenty-first century, the United States was home to an estimated twelve million undocumented immigrants, sometimes called illegal aliens because they are foreigners, or aliens, who do not have permission to be in the country. Most are from Mexico. They cannot become citizens, yet many of them work and pay taxes. Their fate is a problem that the nation has yet to solve.

What is to be done with them? Arrest them and deport them, say those who favor stricter immigration controls or who are against Mexican immigration. Prevent them from getting driver's licenses or jobs. Do not let them use medical services or schools. Build bigger fences and send troops to guard the border. Beneath this nativist speech is a fear of the "browning" of America.

But there is another opinion. *Time* magazine, in its cover story on June 18, 2007, argued that undocumented aliens should be given amnesty. In other words, they should be allowed to stay, no longer as illegals, but with a route to citizenship. Undocumented immigrants are "by their sheer numbers undeportable," the article pointed out. "More important, they are too enmeshed in a healthy U.S. economy to be extracted."

The economic recession that began in 2008, however, showed that the US economy was not healthy. Growth sputtered and unemployment rose. This stressful climate fueled concerns about

undocumented aliens taking jobs or consuming American resources. States such as Arizona and Utah passed laws aimed at cracking down more tightly on illegal immigrants. In 2011 Alabama passed the nation's strictest law, which required schools to check students' immigration status.

Like the earlier waves of Mexican immigrants, new arrivals were being pushed to El Norte by growing poverty. The North American Free Trade Agreement (NAFTA), which became law in 1994, had a devastating effect on Mexican farmers. Under NAFTA, corn grown by US farmers who received financial aid (called subsidies) from the government could be shipped to Mexico, where it was sold more cheaply there than locally grown corn. This bankrupted 1.5 million Mexican farmers.

Many of the ruined farmers fled north across the border. "During the years NAFTA has been in effect," wrote journalist David Bacon in 2007, "more than 6 million people have come to live in the United States. They didn't abandon their homes, families, and farms and jobs willingly. They had no other option for survival."

To cross the border illegally, Mexicans risk death running across busy freeways or walking across parched deserts. They keep coming because they

(left) Demonstrators oppose Alabama's law requiring public schools to check students' immigration status, among other provisions, Birmingham, Alabama, 2011.

know that employers will hire them. Without Mexican labor, many farmers and fruit growers cannot harvest their crops. Ronald Reagan, a Republican who served as US president from 1981 to 1989, was aware of that fact as long ago as 1977, when he pointed out that apples were rotting on the trees of New England because of the lack of workers. "One thing is certain in this hungry world," Reagan said. "[N]o regulation or law should be allowed if it results in crops rotting in the fields for lack of harvesters."

Many of the nation's Mexican immigrants live in California, and the majority of those residents are in the United States legally. In 2006 the US Census Bureau reported that 70 percent of the Mexicans in California were US citizens. Some were born in the United States. Others, born in Mexico, became US citizens through naturalization. One of these naturalized citizens was Roselia Aguilar of San Jose.

Mexican-born Aguilar, who worried about the backlash against Mexican Americans, was twenty-nine years old when she stood with 450 people from fifty-seven nations and solemnly took an oath to "bear true faith and allegiance to the Constitution." Moments after the ceremony she said, "I feel it's one of the most important things that ever happened to me. It's just different. I feel something nice inside me. I feel like I was born again."

YOUNG PEOPLE "COME OUT" AS ILLEGALS

IN 2011 YOUNG PEOPLE ACROSS THE UNITED
states took a stand to raise public awareness of the
plight of students who are "illegals"—foreigners
who do not have the documents that would identify
them as legal immigrants.

Urging lawmakers to pass the DREAM Act,
a proposed path to citizenship for some of the
many young people who were brought into the
United States illegally as children by their parents,
a group called the Dream Team staged a protest
in Charlotte, North Carolina, in September. At a
rally attended by several hundred students, some
stepped forward and announced that they were in
the country illegally. "My name is Alicia Torres and
I'm risking it all," one of them called out. "Today is
the day that I am coming out of the shadows and
saying I exist. I am no longer going to be afraid." At
least ten undocumented immigrants were arrested.

Two months later in Georgia, a recent high-
school graduate named Dulce Guerrera, who had
publicly revealed her own undocumented status
in March, organized a rally at the state capitol for

undocumented high-school students to share their stories with lawmakers.

Youthful activists may have been inspired by a high-profile "coming out." In June 2011 journalist Jose Antonio Vargas, who won a Pulitzer Prize in 2008 for his coverage of a school shooting on the Virginia Tech campus, published an article in the *New York Times* revealing that his mother had sent him from his home in the Philippines to live with his grandparents in the United States when he was twelve. She wanted to give him a better life, but she could not give him immigration documents. For almost twenty years he had lived the life of an illegal alien. He was tired of the secrecy and felt that Americans ought to know how many hard-working, successful people are in his situation.

Opposition to the DREAM Act comes from people like Roy Beck, the director of an organization that pushes for tighter immigration control. He says, "Our own American young adult college grads are in dire straits in the job market. . . . So, as compelling as the case for these DREAM students is, we have to acknowledge that legalizing them does actually victimize our own young adults."

But Vargas, Guerrera, and other activists disagree. They believe there is room in the United

States—and in the American dream—for young people like them: undocumented aliens who had no control over the fact that they were brought into the country illegally. They hope to convince lawmakers to change the immigration rules so that they can become citizens, complete their educations, and look for jobs without having to cover up their origins.

CHAPTER SEVENTEEN

"WE WILL ALL BE MINORITIES"

IN JUNE OF 1997, I was invited to go to the White House to help President Bill Clinton write a speech about race. I was one of a group of civil rights leaders and scholars who met with the president to share ideas on the subject. During the meeting I pointed out that sometime in the twenty-first century, whites will become a minority in the US population. "Yes," I said, "we will all be minorities."

A few days later President Clinton gave the speech, titled "One America in the Twenty-First Century: The President's Initiative on Race," to the graduating class of the University of California at San Diego. "A half-century from now," he told the students, "when your own grandchildren are in college, there will be no majority race in America."

He then presented highlights from our nation's multicultural past:

Consider this: we were born with a Declaration of Independence which asserted that we were all created equal and a Constitution that enshrined slavery. We fought a bloody civil war to abolish slavery and preserve the union, but we remained a house divided and unequal by law for another century. We advanced across the continent in the name of freedom, yet in so doing we pushed Native Americans off their land, often crushing their culture and their livelihood. . . . In World War II, Japanese-Americans fought valiantly for freedom in Europe, taking great casualties, while at home their families were herded into internment camps. The famed Tuskegee Airmen lost none of the bombers they guarded during the war, but their African-American heritage cost them many rights when they came back home in peace. . . .

In his conclusion, Clinton identified the challenge we faced: "Will we become not two, but many Americas, separate, unequal, and isolated? Or will we draw strength from all our people and our ancient faith in the quality of human dignity, to become the world's first truly multi-racial democracy?"

The future is in our hands. The choices we make will be shaped by our view of our own history. A history that leaves out minorities reinforces separation, but a history that includes everyone bridges the divides between groups.

On their voyage through history, the people of America have found their paths crisscrossing one another in events such as Bacon's Rebellion, the Civil War, and World War II. Their lives and cultures have swirled together, from the first meeting of Powhatan Indians and English colonists on the Virginia shore to the latest Mexican immigrants crossing the border. But America's dilemma has been the denial of its diversity.

We originally came from many different shores, and our diversity has been at the center of the making of America. Signs of our ethnic diversity can be found across the land—Ellis Island, Angel Island, Chinatown, Harlem, the Lower East Side, places with Indian names and Spanish names, music with African American origins, and songs such as "White Christmas" written by a Russian Jewish immigrant known as Irving Berlin.

Marginalized minorities have sung "We shall overcome" as they struggled for equality and respect. Their struggle must continue, but they have won a multitude of victories: the abolition of slavery; the integration of the US armed forces and of public schools; the extending of naturalized citizenship to all immigrants regardless of race; the overturning of laws against interracial marriage; apologies to Japanese Americans who were interned during World War II; and the awakening of America to its amazing diversity.

What does the future hold? The promise of the twenty-first century is the promise of the changing colors of the American people. Demography, the study of population trends, is redefining who is an American. White Americans will not be a majority for much longer—America will truly be a nation of minorities.

The time has come for us to embrace our varied selves, because a new America is approaching, a society where diversity is destiny. Woven into our multicultural national story are the heartfelt verse of African American poet Langston Hughes, who wrote,

Let America be America again.

. . . .

Let America be the dream the dreamers dreamed—

. . . .

Equality is in the air we breathe.

Chapter One: Why a Different Mirror?

"the epic story of the great migrations . . ." Oscar Handlin, *The Uprooted: The Epic Story of the Great Migrations that Made the American People* (New York, 1951), p. 3.

"a teeming nation of nations" Walt Whitman, Preface, *Leaves of Grass* (New York, 1958), p. 453.

"We will reach the goal of freedom . . ." Martin Luther King, Jr., *Why We Can't Wait* (New York, 1964), pp. 92–93.

"How could I as a six-month-old child . . ." Congressman Robert Matsui, speech in the House of Representatives, September 17, 1987, Congressional Record (Washington, DC, 1987), p. 7584.

"The white man does not understand . . ." Luther Standing Bear, "What the Indian Means to America," in Wayne Moquin, ed., *Great Documents in American Indian History* (New York, 1973), p. 307.

"are crowding themselves into every place . . ." Leon Litwack, *North of Slavery: The Negro in the Free States, 1790–1860* (Chicago, 1961), p. 163.

"this plentiful country . . ." Arnold Schrier, *Ireland and the American Emigration, 1850–1900* (New York, 1970), p. 24.

"Day of spacious dreams!" Kazuo Ito, *Issei: A History of Japanese Immigrants* (Seattle, 1973), p. 20.

"As the Russians mercilessly . . ." Mark Slobin, *Tenement Songs: The Popular Music of the Jewish Immigrants* (Urbana, IL, 1982), p. 155.

"I don't know why anybody . . ." Hamilton Holt, ed., *The Life Stories of Undistinguished Americans As Told by Themselves* (New York, 1906), p. 143.

"I will tell you something about stories . . ." Leslie Marmon Silko, *Ceremony* (New York, 1978), p. 2.

"[My purpose] is not to tell you . . ." Harriet A. Jacobs, *Incidents in the Life of a Slave Girl* (Cambridge, MA, 1987, originally published 1857), p. xiii.

"realize Chinese people are human" "Social document of Pany Lowe, interviewed by C.H. Burnett, Seattle, July 5, 1924," p. 6, Survey of Race Relations, Stanford University, Hoover Institution Archives.

"the descendants of Lazar and Goldie Glauberman" Minnie Miller, Autobiography, private manuscript, copy from Richard Balkin.

"Let America be America again" Langston Hughes, in Hughes and Arna Bontemps, eds., *The Poetry of the Negro, 1746–1949* (Garden City, NY, 1951), p. 106.

"Down the railroad, um-huh" Mathilde Bunton, "Negro Work Songs" (1940), typescript in Box 91 ("Music"), Illinois Writers Projects, USWPA, in James R. Grossman's *Land of Hope: Chicago, Black Sojourners, and the Great Migration* (Chicago, 1989). p. 182.

"Then drill, my Paddies, drill" Carl Wittke, *The Irish in America* (Baton Rouge, LA, 1956), p. 39.

"A railroad worker. . ." Ito, p. 343.

"Some unloaded rails" Manuel Gamio, *Mexican Immigration to the United States* (Chicago, 1930), pp. 84–85.

Chapter Two: Removing the "Savages"

"Nothing but fear and force" Nicholas P. Canny, "The Ideology of English Colonization: From Ireland to America," *William and Mary Quarterly*, 3rd series, vol., 30, no. 4 (October 1973), pp. 593, 582.

"was showed up and down London . . ." Robert R. Cawley, "Shakespeare's Use of the Voyages in The Tempest," *Publications of the Modern Language Association of America*, vol. 41, no. 3 (September 1926), pp, 720, 721.

"train them up with gentleness . . ." George Frederickson, *White Supremacy: A Comparative Study in American & South African History* (New York, 1971), p. 12.

"the starving time . . . fury of the savages" In Mortimer J. Adler, ed., *Annals of America, vol. 1, Discovering a New World* (Chicago, 1968), pp. 21, 26.

"throwing them overboard . . ." Kirkpatrick Sale, *The Conquest of Paradise: Christopher Columbus and the Columbian Legacy* (New York, 1990), p. 277.

"brought home parts of their heads" Sale, p. 294.

"root out [the Indians] . . ." Francis Jennings, *The Invasion of America: Indians, Colonialism, and the Cant of Conquest* (New York, 1976), p. 153.

"all planted with corn . . ." Howard S. Russell, *Indian New England Before the Mayflower* (Hanover, NH, 1980), p. 11.

"For it pleased God . . ." in Carolyn Merchant, *Ecological Revolutions: Nature, Gender, and Science in New England* (Chapel Hill, NC, 1989), p. 90.

"I did not see . . ." David R. Ford, "Mary Rowlandson's Captivity Narrative: A Paradigm of Puritan Representations of Native Americans?" Ethnic Studies 299 paper, fall 1996, University of California, Berkeley.

"[T]he times have turned everything . . ." James Axtell, *The Invasion Within: The Contest of Cultures in Colonial North America* (New York, 1985), p. 167.

"both Americans . . ." in Andrew Lipscomb and Albert E. Bergh, eds., *Writings of Thomas Jefferson* (Washington, DC, 1904), vol., 16, p. 372.

"Nothing will reduce those wretches . . ." Lipscomb and Bergh, vol. 4, pp. 270–271.

"I shall rejoice . . ." Lipscomb and Bergh, vol. 16, p. 434.

"Your lands are your own . . ." Lipscomb and Bergh, vol. 16, pp. 401, 429.

"wild beasts . . . civilization" Lipscomb and Bergh, vol. 16, pp. 74–75.

"During my adoption . . ." James E. Seaver, *A Narrative of the Life of Mrs. Mary Jemison*, 1823, online at Project Gutenberg.

Chapter Three: The Hidden Origins of Slavery

"English servants running . . ." Abbot Emerson Smith, *Colonists in Bondage: White Servitude and Convict Labor in America, 1607–1776* (Gloucester, MA, 1965), p. 253.

"Poor Indebted . . ." T.H. Breen, "A Changing Labor Force and Race Relations in Virginia, 1660–1710," *Journal of Social History*, vol. 7, Fall 1973, pp. 3–4.

"prevent or suppress . . ." Breen, "Changing Labor Force," p. 12.

"to see an abolition . . ." Thomas Jefferson to Brissot de Warville, February 11, 1788, in Julian Boyd, ed., *The Papers of Thomas Jefferson*, 18 vols. (Princeton, 1950–1965), vol. 12, pp. 577–578.

"Deep-rooted prejudices . . ." Thomas Jefferson, *Notes on the State of Virginia* (New York, 1861), pp. 132–133.

"As it is . . ." Thomas Jefferson to John Holmes, April 22, 1820, in Paul L. Ford, ed., *The Works of Thomas Jefferson, 20 vols.* (New York, 1892–1899), vol. 13, p. 159.

"The first object . . ." Olaudah Equiano, "Early Travels of Olaudah Equiano," in Philip D. Curtain, *Africa Remembered: Narratives by West Africans from the Era of the Slave Trade* (Madison, WI, 1968), pp. 92–97.

Chapter Four: The Road to the Reservation

"savage bloodhounds . . ." Michael Paul Rogin, *Fathers and Children: Andrew Jackson and the Subjugation of the American Indian* (New York, 1975), pp. 140–141.

"These fiends . . ." Andrew Jackson, Proclamation, April 2, 1814, Fort Williams, in John Spencer Bassett, ed., *Correspondence of Andrew Jackson, 6 vols.*, (Washington, DC, 1926), vol. 1, p. 494.

"to be guaranteed . . ." Andrew Jackson, Speech to the Chicksaws, in James D. Richardson, ed., *A Compilation of the Messages and Papers of the Presidents, 1789–1897* (Washington, DC, 1897), vol. 2, p. 241.

"red children" Jackson, Speech to the Chickasaws.

"It is the voice . . ." Arthur H. DeRosier Jr., *The Removal of Choctaw Indians* (New York, 1972), p. 104.

"It was then the middle . . ." Alexis de Toqueville, *Democracy in America, 2 vols.* (New York, 1945), vol. 1, pp. 352–353.

"We were hedged in . . ." Angie Debo, *The Rise and Fall of the Choctaw Republic* (Norman, OK, 1972), p. 56; Wayne Moquin, ed., *Great Documents in American Indian History* (New York, 1973), pp. 151–153.

"Looks like maybe . . ." Thurman Wilkins, *Cherokee Tragedy: The Story of the Ridge Family and of the Decimation of a People* (New York, 1970), p. 314.

"In a few years . . ." "The Spirit of the Times; or the Fast Age," *Democratic Review*, vol. 33 (September 1853), pp. 260–261.

"What shall we . . ." Alfred L. Riggs, "What Shall We Do With the Indians?" *The Nation*, vol. 67, October 31, 1867), p. 356.

"no Indian nation or tribe . . ." Francis Amasa Walker, *The Indian Question* (Boston, 1874), p. 5.

"To do what they . . ." Martha Royce Blaine, *Pawnee Passage: 1870–1875* (Norman, OK, 1990), p. 143.

"Long time we travel . . ." Thurman Wilkins, *Cherokee Tragedy: The Story of the Ridge Family and of the Decimation of a People* (New York, 1970), p. 314.

Carrie Bushyhead . . . Details from Famous Cherokee from the Historical Eras, http://www.aaanativearts.com/cherokee/famous-cherokee.htm, Oklahoma Geneaological Society, and her grave marker, which can be viewed online at http://www.findagrave.com/cgi-bin/fg.cgi?page=gr&GRid=5647172

Chapter Five: Life in Slavery

"Masters want us . . ." David Walker, *An Appeal to the Colored Citizens of the World* (New York, 1965), p. 34.

"No one will employ . . ." Leon Litwack, *North of Slavery: The Negro in the Free States, 1790–1860* (Chicago, 1965), p. 154.

"The hands are required . . ." Kenneth M. Stampp, *The Peculiar Institution: Slavery in the Ante-bellum South* (New York, 1956), p. 44.

"We have to rely . . ." Stampp, p. 146.

"the bloody scenes . . ." Frederick Douglass, *Narrative of the Life of Frederick Douglass* (New York, 1968; originally published 1845), p. 26.

"They left without . . ." Leon Litwack, *Been in the Storm So Long: The Aftermath of Slavery* (New York, 1979), p. 144.

"I believe it is the policy . . ." Joel Williamson, *After Slavery: The Negro in South Carolina during Reconstruction, 1861–1877* (Chapel Hill, NC, 1965), p. 54.

"Wretched woman!" "Mr. Loguen's reply," Junius P. Rodriguez, ed., *Slavery in the United States: A Social, Political, and Historical Encyclopedia* (Santa Barbara, CA, 2007), p. 678.

Chapter Six: The Flight from Ireland

"extremely poor . . . dirty Hovels . . ." Owen Dudley Edwards, "The American Image of Ireland: A Study of Its Early Phases," *Perspectives in American History*, vol. 4 (1970), p. 236.

"famished and ghastly . . ." Kerby A. Miller, *Emigrants and Exiles: Ireland and the Irish Exodus to North America* (New York, 1985), p. 285.

"immortal Irish brigade . . ." Carl Wittke, *The Irish in America* (Baton Rouge, 1956), pp. 32–33.

"despised and . . ." Miller, *Emigrants and Exiles*, p. 318.

"I got a letter . . ." Kerby A. Miller, "Assimilation and Alienation: Irish Emigrants' Responses to Industrial America, 1871-1921," in P.J. Drudy, ed., *Irish in America* (Cambridge, MA, 1985), p. 105.

"American labor . . . Chinese standard . . ." Frederick Rudolph, "Chinamen in Yankeedom: Anti-Unionism in Massachusetts in 1870," *American Historical Review*, vol. 53, no. 1 (October 1947), p. 10.

"inferior . . . lower . . .negroes . . ." Stanley K. Schultz, *The Culture Factory: Boston Public Schools, 1789–1860* (New York, 1973), p. 243.

"country of the whites" David R. Roediger, *The Wages of Whiteness: Race and the Making of the American Working Class* (London, 1991), p.137.

"It is to be regretted . . ." Gilbert Osofsky, *Harlem: The Making of a Ghetto, Negro New York, 1890–1930* (New York, 1966), p. 45.

"steal the work . . ." Adrian Cook, *Armies of the Streets: The New York City Draft Riots of 1863* (Lexington, KY, 1974), p. 205.

"What I minded . . ." Helen Campbell, *Prisoners of Poverty: Women Wage-Workers, Their Trades and Their Lives* (Boston, 1900), p. 226.

"No female . . . " Arnold Schreier, *Ireland and the American Emigration, 1850–1900* (New York, 1970), p. 28.

"this is . . ." Schreier, p. 24.

"I am getting along . . ." Schreier, p. 38.

"The second generation . . ." Miller, *Emigrants and Exiles*, p. 508.

Mother Jones and the Children's Crusade . . . Sources: Simon Cordery, *Mother Jones: Raising Cain and Consciousness* (Albuquerque, NM, 2010); Elliott J. Gorn, *Mother Jones: The Most Dangerous Woman in America* (New York, 2002).

"After a long and weary march . . ." Mary Harris (Mother) Jones, "The Wail of the Children," Joseph J. Fahey and Richard Armstrong, eds., *A Peace Reader: Essential Readings on War, Justice, Non-Violence and World Order, rev. ed.* (Mahwah, NJ, 1992), p. 138

Chapter Seven: The War Against Mexico

"In my judgment . . ." David J. Weber, ed., *Foreigners in Their Native Land: Historical Roots of the Mexican Americans* (Albuquerque, NM, 1973), p. 102.

"mongrel . . ." Rodolfo Acuña, *Occupied America: A History of Chicanos* (New York, 1981), p. 6–7.

"War is our only . . ." Acuña, p. 8.

"War exists . . ." Weber, p. 95.

"an extensive and profitable . . ." James K. Polk, in Norman Graeber, *Empire on the Pacific: A Study in American Continental Expansion* (New York, 1955), p. 50.

"Since we have been in Matamoros . . ." Acuña, p. 15.

"committed atrocities . . ." Carey McWilliams, *North from Mexico: The Spanish-Speaking People of the United States* (New York, 1968), p. 102.

"What has miserable . . ." Reginald Horsman, *Race and Manifest Destiny: The Origins of American Racial Anglo-Saxonism* (Cambridge, MA, 1981), p. 235.

"Descendants of the Indians . . ." Acuña, p. 20.

"conquered . . . foreigners . . ." Weber, p. 176.

"The Spanish people had . . ." Albert Camarillo, *Chicanos in a Changing Society: From Mexican Pueblos to American Barrios in Santa Barbara and Southern California, 1849–1930* (Cambridge, MA, 1979), p. 36.

"Mexicans have sold . . ." David Montejano, *Anglos and Mexicans in the Making of Texas, 1836–1986* (Austin, TX, 1987), p. 113.

"the lower class of Mexicans . . ." Andres E. Jimenez Montoya, "Political Discrimination in the Labor Market: Racial Division in the Arizona Copper Industry," Working Paper 103, Institute for the Study of Social Change, University of California, Berkeley (1977), p. 20.

"We beg to say . . ." Tomas Almaguer, "Racial Domination and Class Conflict in Capitalist Agriculture: The Oxnard Sugar Beet Workers' Strike of 1903," *Labor History*, vol. 25, no. 3 (Summer 1984), p. 346.

"The language now spoken . . ." M.G. Vallejo, "What the Gold Rush Brought to California," Valeska Bari, ed., *The Course of Empire: First Hand Accounts of California in the Days of the Gold Rush of '49* (New York, 1931), p. 53.

Chapter Eight: From China to Gold Mountain

"White men and women . . ." Carey McWilliams, *Factories in the Field* (Santa Barbara, CA, 1971), p. 74.

"Chinese and other people not white" California Supreme Court, *The People v. Hall*, October 1, 1854, in Robert F. Heizer and Alan F. Almquist, *The Other Californians: Prejudice and Discrimination under Spain, Mexico, and the United States to 1920* (Berkeley, CA, 1971), p. 229.

"Our experience . . ." Stuart C. Miller, *The Unwelcome Immigrant: The American Image of the Chinese, 1752–1882* (Berkeley, CA, 1969), p. 190.

"The Chinese were in a pitiable state . . ." Huie Kin, *Reminiscences* (Peiping, 1932), p. 27.

"The greatest impression . . ."

"There was endless discussion . . ." Victor Wong, "Childhood II," in Nick Harvey, ed., *Ting: The Cauldron: Chinese Art and Identity in San Francisco* (San Francisco, 1970), p. 71. "Yes, well, we had a dog . . ." Shih-shan Henry Tsai, *The Chinese Experience in America* (Bloomington, IN, 1986), p. 101.

Chapter Nine: Dealing with the Indians

"the meeting point . . ." Frederick Jackson Turner, "The Significance of the Frontier in American History," in *The Early Writings of Frederick Jackson Turner* (Madison, WI, 1939), p. 185.

"All Indians must dance . . ." James Mooney, The Ghost-Dance Religion and the Sioux Outbreak of 1890, Fourteenth Annual Report of the Bureau of Ethnology, 1892–1892, Part 2 (Washington, DC, 1896), p. 26.

"Indians are dancing . . ." Dee Brown, *Bury My Heart at Wounded Knee: An Indian History of the American West* (New York, 1970), p. 436.

"There were only . . ." Black Elk, Black Elk Speaks: Being the Life Story of a Holy Man of the Oglala Sioux, as told to John G. Neihardt (Lincoln, NE, 1961), pp. 161–162.

"Dead and wounded . . ." Black Elk, p. 259.

"free and open plains . . ." George A. Custer, *Wild Life on the Plains and Horrors of Indian Warfare* (St. Louis, 1891), pp. 139–140

"eventually open to settlement . . ." Francis Prucha, *Americanizing the American Indians: Writings by the "Friends of the Indian":* *1800–1900* (Cambridge, MA, 1973), p.108.

"it will be but a few years . . ." Hoxie, p. 160.

"If the Indian life . . ." John Collier, *From Every Zenith: A Memoir and Some Essays on Life and Thought* (Denver, 1963), p. 203.

"In my long life . . ." Collier, p. 252.

"You people are indeed . . ." Peter Nabokov, ed., *Native American Testimony* (New York, 1978), p. 330.

"Take the handle . . .. wisely kept." Frederick E. Hoxie, *A Final Promise: The Campaign to Assimilate the Indians, 1880–1920* (Lincoln, NE, 1984), p. 180.

Chapter Ten: The Japanese and "Money Trees"

"In America . . ." Kazuo Ito, *Issei: A History of the Japanese Immigrants in North America* (Seattle, 1973), p. 29.

"Huge dreams . . ." p. 38.

"Don't stay . . . twenty years." Eileen Sunada Sarasohn, ed., *The Issei: Portrait of a Pioneer, an Oral History* (Palo Alto, CA, 1983), 34.

"Keep a variety . . ." G.C. Hewitt to W.G. Irwin and Company, March 18, 1896, Hutchinson Plantation Records.

"I haven't got . . ." Machiyo Mitamura, "Life on a Hawaiian Plantation: An Interview," in *Social Process in Hawaii*, vol. 6 (1940), p. 51.

"If we talked too much . . ." Ethnic Studies Oral History Project, *Uchinanchu: A History of Okinawans in Hawaii* (Honolulu, 1981), p. 513.

"My husband cuts . . ." Song, in Yukuo Uyehara, "The Horehore-Bushi: A Type of Japanese Folksong Developed and Sung Among the Early Immigrants in Hawaii," *Social Process in Hawaii*, vol. 28 (1980–1981), p. 114.

"unite our destiny . . ." Letter to plantation manager E. K. Bull, signed by ninety-two strikers, May 19, 1909, reprinted in Bureau of Labor Statistics, Report of the Commissioner of Labor on Hawaii (Washington, 1910), p. 80.

"laborers of all nationalities" Takashi Tsutsumi, *History of Hawaii Laborers' Movement* (Honolulu, 1922), p. 22.

"Pleasant surroundings . . ." Donald S. Bowman, "Housing the Plantation Worker," *The Hawaiian Planter's Record*, vol. 22, no. 4 (April 1920), p. 202–203.

"The language we used . . ." Ethnic Studies Oral History Project, *Waialua and Haleiwa: The People Tell Their Story* (Honolulu, 1977), vol.3, p. 11.

"With one woven basket . . ." Song, *Hawaii Herald*, February 2, 1973.

"But I didn't realize . . ." William C. Smith, *The Second Generation Oriental in America* (Honolulu, 1927), p. 21.

"America . . . once . . ." Ito, p. 889.

"I would much rather . . ." "Interview with Miss Esther B. Bartlett of Y.W.C.A.," December 12, 1925, p. 5, Survey of Race Relations, Stanford University. Hoover Institution Library.

"When I told my parents . . . All agreed to our marriage . . ." Eileen Sunada Sarasohn, ed. *The Issei: Portrait of a Pioneer, an Oral History* (Palo Alto, CA, 1983), p. 44, pp. 31–32.

Chapter Eleven: Jews Are Pushed from Russia

"It was not easy to live . . ." Irving Howe, *World of Our Fathers: The Journey of the East European Jews to America and the Life They Found and Made* (New York, 1983), p. 10.

"I feel that every cobblestone . . ." Sydelle Kramer and Jenny Masur, eds. *Jewish Grandmothers* (Boston, 1976), p. 64.

"This was the point . . ." Abraham Cahan, *The Education of Abraham Cahan*, translated by Leon Stein, Abraham P. Conan, and Lynn Davison (Philadelphia, 1969), p. 188.

"Everyone was on deck . . ." Ronald Sanders, *Shores of Refuge: A Hundred Years of Jewish Emigration* (New York, 1988), p. 161.

"My work was . . ." Milton Meltzer, *Taking Root: Jewish Immigrants in America* (New York, 1976), pp. 111–112.

"I looked upon the dead bodies . . ." Elizabeth Ewen, *Immigrant Women in the Land of Dollars: Life and Culture on the Lower East Side, 1890–1925* (New York, 1985), p. 260.

"By the end of World War I . . . " Susan A. Glenn, *Daughters of the Shtetl: Life and Labor in the Immigrant Generation* (Ithaca, NY, 1990), p. 169.

"During the few years . . ." Ewen, p. 72.

"more dirty Jews . . ." Stephen Steinberg, *The Ethnic Myth: Race, Ethnicity, and Class in America* (New York, 1981), p. 234.

"All of us under . . ." Mayor James Curley, in Marcia Graham Synnott, *The Half-Opened Door: Discrimination and Admissions at Harvard, Yale, and Princeton, 1900–1970* (Westport, CT, 1979), p. 112.

"I am a working girl . . ." Clara Lemlich, in Howe, p. 298, and Howard M. Sachar, *A History of the Jews in America* (New York, 1992), p. 183. Additional information about Clara Lemlich from Annelise Orleck, "Clara Lemlich Shavelson," Jewish Women: A Comprehensive Historical Encyclopedia, Jewish Women's Archive, online at http://jwa.org/encyclopedia/article/shavelson-clara-lemlich

Chapter Twelve: Up from Mexico

"All you had to do . . ." Mario T. Garcia, *Desert Immigrants: The Mexicans of El Paso, 1880–1920* (New Haven, CT, 1981), p. 37.

"If anyone has any doubt . . ." Ricardo Romo, *East Lost Angeles: History of a Barrio* (Austin, TX, 1983), p. 45.

"We came to the United States . . ." Romo, p. 6.

"There is not a day . . ." David J. Weber, *Foreigners in Their Native Land: Historical Roots of the Mexican Americans* (Albuquerque, NM, 1973), p. 260.

"The fleeting engine . . ." Manuel Gamio, *Mexican Immigration to the United States*, (Chicago, 1930), pp. 91–92.

"His strongest point . . ." Garcia, p. 68.

"They have finished . . ." Mark Reisler, *By the Sweat of Their Brow: Mexican Immigrant Labor in the United States, 1900–1940* (Westport, CT, 1976), p. 85.

"We protect our farmers . . ." Reisler, p. 240.

"Well, we believe . . ." Devra A. Weber, "Mexican Women on Strike: Memory, History, and Oral Narrative," in Adelaida R. Del Castillo, ed., *Between Borders: Essays on Mexicana/Chicana History* (Encino, CA, 1990), p. 192.

"I have left . . ." Gamio, p. 147.

"Two years ago . . ." "Interview with Inder Singh," Survey of Race Relations, Stanford University, Hoover Institution Archives, p. 1.

"There would be a revolution . . ." David Montejano, *Anglos and Mexicans in the Making of Texas, 1936–1986* (Austin, TX, 1987), pp. 226-227.

"Educated Mexicans . . ." Rosalinda M. Gonzalez, "Chicanas and Mexican Immigrant Families, 1920–1940: Women's Subordination and Family Exploitation," in Lois Scharf and Joan M. Jenson, eds., *Decades of Discontent: The Women's Movement, 1920–1940* (Westport, CT, 1983), p. 66.

"Your people are here . . ." Garcia, p. 125.

"Becoming a proud American . . ." Ernesto Galarza, *Barrio Boy: The Story of a Boy's Acculturation* (Notre Dame, IN, 1971), p. 211.

"From the racial . . ." Reisler, p. 155.

"My mother was left . . ." Ignacio Piña details and quotes from Wendy Koch, "U.S. urged to apologize for 1930s deportations," *USA Today*, April 5, 2006, online at http://www.usatoday.com/news/nation/2006-04-04-1930s-deportees-cover_x.htm

Chapter Thirteen: Blacks Arrive in Northern Cities

"And Black men's feet . . ." Zora Neale Hurston, *Jonah's Gourd Vine* (New York, 1990, originally published in 1934), pp. 147–148.

"Where I come from . . ." Gilbert Osofsky, *Harlem: The Making of a Ghetto, Negro New York, 1890–1930* (New York, 1965), p. 23.

"The best wages . . ." Ray Stannard Baker, "The Negro Goes North," *World's Work*, vol. 34 (July 1917), p. 315.

"He came home . . ." Baker, p. 314.

"discontented . . ." Osofsky, pp. 24–25.

"Why stay in the South . . ." Emmett J. Scott, *Negro Migration During the War* (London, 1920), p. 33.

"The districts . . ." Allan H. Spear, *Black Chicago: The Making of a Negro Ghetto, 1890–1920* (Chicago, 1967), p. 202.

"pouring into Chicago . . ." Spear, p. 209.

"unite all labor . . ." Raymond Wolters, *Negroes and the Great Depression: The Problem of Economic Recovery* (Westport, CT, 1970), p. 250.

"Up, you mighty race . . . " E. David Cronon, *Black Moses: The Story of Marcus Garvey and the Universal Negro Improvement Association* (Madison, WI, 1966), p. 70.

"To me, at home . . . It was then . . ." Marcus Garvey, "The Negro's Greatest Enemy," *Current History*, vol. 18 (September 1923), p. 951–953.

"If Europe is for the Europeans . . ." Cronon, p. 65.

"Garvey made thousands think . . ." Cronon, p. 136.

Chapter Fourteen: World War II and America's Ethnic Problem

"There is no intention . . ." Personal Justice Denied: Commission on Wartime Relocation and Internment of Civilians (Washington, DC, 1982), p. 265.

"principles that gave . . . Mike Cohen, Jewish." Adam Clayton Powell, Jr., Marching Blacks (New York, 1945), p. 125.

"To men of my generation . . ." Victor G. and Brett de Bary Nee, Longtime Californ': A Documentary Study of an American China-town (San Francisco, 1972), pp. 154–155.

"In the 1940s . . ." Diane Mark and Ginger Chih, A Place Called Chinese America (Dubuque, IA, 19820, pp. 97–98

"All of us . . ." Robert Haro, interview, July 25, 1988.

"I remember one day . . ." Richard Santillán, "Rosita the Riveter: Midwest Mexican American Women During World War II," Perspectives in Mexican American Studies, vol. 2 (1989), p. 128.

"Our answer is . . ." Jere Franco, "Bringing Them Alive: Selective Service and Native Americans," Journal of Ethnic Studies, vol. 18, no. 3 (Fall 1990), p. 18.

"The marines recruited Navajos . . ." Cozy Stanley Brown, interview, in Broderick H. Johnson, ed., Navajos and World War II (Tsaile, Navajo Nation, AZ, 1977), p. 54.

"unbreakable code" Isabel Simmons, "The Unbreakable Code," Marine Corps Gazette, November 1971.

"Without the Navajos . . ." Bruce Watson, "Navajo Code Talkers: A Few Good Men," Smithsonian, vol. 24, no. 5 (August 1993), p. 40.

"When I was going . . ." Kenji Kawano, Warriors: Navajo Code Talkers (Flagstaff, AZ, 1990), p. 16.

"Japs—savages . . ." Harry Truman, Diary, in Robert H. Ferrell, ed., *Off the Record: The Private Papers of Harry S. Truman* (New York, 1982), p. 53.

"for democracy . . ." Francis L. Broderick, *W. E. B. Du Bois: Negro Leader in a Time of Crisis* (Stanford, CA, 1966), p. 196.

"DEAR EDITOR: . . ." James Thompson, reprinted in Philip McGuire, ed., *Taps for a Jim Crow Army: Letters from Black Soldiers in World War II* (Lexington, KY, 1993), pp. 19–20; see also PBS, *Soldiers Without Swords: The Black Press*, "Newspapers: The Pittsburgh Courier," online at http://www.pbs.org/blackpress/news_bios/courier.html and Andrew Buni, *Robert L. Vann of the Pittsburgh Courier: Politics and Black Journalism* (Pittsburgh, 1974).

Chapter Fifteen: Calls for Change

"Negroes are in no mood . . ." Philip McGuire, ed., *Taps for a Jim Crow Army: Letters from Black Soldiers in World War II* (Lexington, KY, 1993), p. 248.

"outright racial discrimination" US Supreme Court, *Oyama v. California*, 332 (US) 633, 1948, online at http://caselaw.lp.findlaw.com/scripts/getcase.pl?court=US&vol=332&invol=633

"Going steadily to study . . ." Kiyoko Nieda, in Lucille Nixon and Tomoe Tana, eds. and trans., *Sounds from the Unknown: A Collection of Japanese-American Tanka* (Denver, 1963), p. 49.

"utterly loyal . . .a sad chapter . . ." *San Francisco Chronicle*, August 11, 1988.

"We knew this was . . ." Juana Caudillo, in Richard Santillán, "Midwestern Mexican American Women and the Struggle for Gender Equality," Perspectives in Modern Mexican American Studies, vol. 5 (1995), p. 98.

"When our young men . . ." Eva Hernandez, in Santillán, p. 138.

"I myself desegregated . . ." Quoted by James Farmer, in Francis L. Broderick and August Meier, *Negro Protest Thought in the Twentieth Century* (New York, 1965), p. 372.

"Five score years ago . . ." Martin Luther King, Jr., "I Have a Dream," in Broderick and Meier, pp. 400–405.

"I don't see . . ." James H. Cone, *Martin & Malcolm & America: A Dream or a Nightmare* (Maryknoll, NY, 1991), p. 1.

"The Rodney King riots . . . related to one another." Richard Rodriquez, "Horizontal City," This World, *San Francisco Chronicle,* May 24, 1992, p. 16.

"We would go after school . . ." Ellen Levine, *Freedom's Children: Young Civil Rights Activists Tell Their Own Stories* (New York, 2000).

Chapter Sixteen: New Waves of Newcomers

"Just as we sought . . ." David Reimers, *Still the Golden Door: The Third World Comes to America* (New York, 1985), pp. 67–83.

"The conditions in the factories . . ." Alexander Reid, "New Asian Immigrants, New Garment Center," *New York Times,* October 5, 1986.

"Life was very hard . . ." Lesleyanne Hawthorne, *Refugee: The Vietnamese Experience,* (Melbourne, Australia, 1982), p. 237.

"Remember these are people . . ." Alan Hope, "Language, Culture Are Biggest Hurdles for Vietnamese," *Gainesville Times* (GA), March 31, 1985.

"The Taliban are . . ." Jonathan Curiel, "Afghan Angst: Bay Area Community Watches Taliban Depredations from Afar," *San Francisco Chronicle,* March 18, 2001.

"It was at this moment . . ." Nadeem Saeed, email to Professor Ronald Takaki, September 11, 2007.

"I started hearing . . . what integration means." Fatema Nourzaie, email to Professor Ronald Takaki, September 15, 2007.

"The 2010 census . . ." Haya El Nasser and Paul Overberg, "Census shows growth among Asian Indians," *USA Today,*

May 17, 2011, online at http://www.usatoday.com/news/nation/ census/2011-05-12-asian-indian-population-Census_n.htm

"by their sheer numbers . . ." "Immigration: Why Amnesty Makes Sense," *Time*, June 18, 2007, p. 42.

"During the years . . ." David Bacon, "What a Vote for Free Trade Means for the U.S.," *San Francisco Chronicle*, November 20, 2007.

"One thing is certain . . ." Ronald Reagan, quoted in Fareed Zakaria, "America's New Know-Nothings," *Newsweek*, May 28, 2007, p. 39.

"My name is . . ." Franco Ordoñez, "Immigrants arrested at Charlotte 'coming out' rally," *Rock Hill Herald*, September 7, 2011, online at http://www.heraldonline.com/2011/09/07/3346765/ immigrants-arrested-at-charlotte.html

"Our own American . . ." Kate Brumback, "Illegal immigrant youth, like journalist Vargas, 'come out' in reform push," *Denver Post*, June 23, 2011, online at http://www.denverpost.com/break-ingnews/ci 18339986

Chapter Seventeen: "We Will All Be Minorities"

"A half-century from now . . . truly multicultural democracy." President Bill Clinton, "One America in the Twenty-First Century: The President's Initiative on Race" (Washington, DC, White House, 1997).

"Let America be . . ." Langston Hughes, "Let America Be America Again," in Langston Hughes and Arna Bontemps, eds., *The Poetry of the Negro, 1746–1949* (Garden City, NY, 1951), p. 106.

GLOSSARY

abolition ending or doing away with something; in American history, usually refers to the movement to abolish or end slavery

amnesty a government's or other authority's decision to pardon a group of people for an act committed in the past

assimilation the process of blending in among, or taking on the characteristics of, a larger group

communist supporter of communism, a political and economic system in which the state owns the means of economic production, such as factories and farmland, and manages the economy; nineteenth-century German thinker Karl Marx developed the political theory that views a communist society without classes or states as the outcome of human political and economic development

discrimination unequal or unfair treatment of individuals or whole groups based on features such as race, gender, ethnic origin, or religion; treatment based on prejudice

elite group that has superior status in a society, due to political power, wealth, or inherited noble rank

ethnicity quality of belonging to an ethnic group, a population that shares the same national, racial, cultural, or tribal background

executive order an order, regulation, or instruction issued by the head of an executive branch of government, such as a president, governor, or mayor

exploit to take advantage of

fascism belief that national identity should be equal to shared ethnic identity, and that a nation consists of people with the same ancestry, culture, religion, or values; the fascist idea that people or groups outside the shared identity weaken the nation can lead to prejudice or violence against minorities; in politics, fascism usually takes the form of authoritarian governments with a single all-powerful party or leader, such as Benito Mussolini of Italy and Adolf Hitler of Germany during World War II

federal having to do with the central or national level of government and its powers and responsibilities

genocide an organized effort to eliminate a particular racial, ethnic, religious, or cultural group

ghetto place set aside by law or custom to be inhabited by a specific group who may be unable to live outside the ghetto for legal or economic reasons; originally referred to the part of the Italian city of Venice where Jews were required to live, later used for the Jewish sections of cities throughout Europe; some ghettos were ancient neighborhoods where Jews lived together by choice, but many were segregated quarters created by authorities and laws that forced Jews to live apart from the rest of society

integration mixing together; in American history, usually refers to the end of laws that separated, or segregated, people by race; integration was brought about by the civil rights movement and laws of the mid-twentieth century

internment the act of confining a specific group of people away from the general population, by military force or by law

lynching racially based murder; in American history, usually refers to the illegal killing of black people, mostly men, by whites

militia citizens who are not soldiers but who possess weapons and are prepared for military service in an emergency

nationalism belief that one's own nation or culture is superior to others, or the act of setting the interests of one's nation or culture above others

nativism policies that favor native-born inhabitants over immigrants, or the belief that native-born citizens are superior to immigrants

naturalized citizen foreign-born person who becomes a citizen through legal means

pogrom organized massacre of helpless people, often used to refer to massacres of Jewish people

segregation separation; in American history, usually refers to the separation of races under law

speculation buying a quantity of something, such as land, not to use but in the hope of reselling it within a short time at a profit

stereotype an idea or image of what a particular kind of person is like, based on opinions or feelings, not necessarily on facts or experience

suffrage the right to vote

treason the crime of trying to overthrow or attack one's own government